Contents

For Your Consideration

This book has been made for you and, if you so choose, about you. The chapters have been designed to offer you insights that will lead you to a happier, more fulfilling life. Additionally, if you choose to answer the questions within and at the end of each chapter, then you will create a much more personalized—and meaningful—*Life* strategy for yourself. Enjoy your journey.

Journeying From Structured Living to Free Choice

"The unexamined life is not worth living." — Socrates

Debt, divorce, and disappointment await the average graduate with average thoughts. The average American marriage ends in divorce. The average American household owes thousands of dollars to credit card companies. Other facts, which we shall soon explore, also paint a gloomy picture of what a typical graduate's life will be like at age 30. Fortunately, we do not have to be "typical." By rising above the average societal ways of thinking we can achieve happier, more fulfilling lives. Similarly, by using non-average methods of choosing we can increase our control of the future.

We can gain more control of our futures because, when we graduate, we still possess the potential to achieve almost any goal. Sadly, without realizing it, many of us trade this potential away. Our transition from structured school routines to the "real world" of freely chosen jobs and relationships excites us, yet it also distracts us from developing four of our most powerful controls. If we do not build up these controls, then we will slowly surrender our future life options. Without options, we will feel as though we have become a powerless pawn in somebody else's game. Listening to a group of 30 year-olds complain about working at boring jobs for bosses that they dislike helps us understand how quickly we can lose our graduation dreams of happy fulfillment.

Rather than slipping into a typical future of regret, let us make some intelligent choices now, build up our controls, and enjoy prosperous lives.

An Intelligent, Principled Approach to Life's Decisions

What is intelligence? How would you recognize it? Various dictionaries offer you answers that are based upon a person's ability to show judgment and comprehension. For myself, having been biased by my military, martial arts, business, and academic experiences, I prefer a results-oriented description inspired largely from the writings of Jeff Hawkins's book, *On Intelligence.* For the purpose of this *Life-Altering* journey, intelligence shall be defined as "*the ability to accurately predict*." Experience has shown that one of the key differences between successful and unsuccessful people is the ability to reasonably predict how a set of actions will lead to certain outcomes. Military generals and individual fighters who anticipate their opponents' moves earn battle success. Business people who anticipate their customers' needs earn sales success. Across all fields of life, success is associated with those who have the intelligent ability to "see" how choices lead to results.

Given this definition of intelligence, can we really be so bold as to say that there is an "intelligent" approach to making many of life's major decisions? Yes! Centuries of research have produced a large body of knowledge that offers a fairly reliable set of predictions about the *Life-Altering Choices* that you will encounter during your 20s. This research also predicts how the various *Choices* will likely lead you to fulfilling, or disappointing, outcomes.

Did you notice that I wrote "predicts," and not "guarantees?" Too often, people will try to sell you guaranteed solutions, but their techniques only work in very specific situations. For example, I once trained at a martial arts school where new students were taught a specific blocking move so that they could stop a specific punch. That technique would certainly have been useful if the students ever had that specific punch thrown at them. However, since there are hundreds of ways that an opponent can throw a punch at you, being taught a specific technique actually offers you relatively little value—your technique will be useless against many of the other attacks that you may encounter.

Rather than teaching specific techniques, some martial arts teachers train their students with general concepts, such as "do not meet force with force," or "get out of the way first." This way, no matter how a punch—or kick—is thrown at them, students may apply their principles to survive an attack and then respond with a counterattack principle, such as a destabilization move.

I believe that this same principled approach should be taken with *Life-Altering Choices*. To better understand why, please try the following experiment...

Pick any set of interests, such as:

Romance	Career	God	Exercise	Friends
Dating	Car	House	Clothes	Love
Pets	Marriage	Sex	Dining Out	Learning
Retirement	Vacationing	Parents	Relaxing	Movies

...and list them on a sheet of paper in their order of importance to you.

Next, perform one or both of the following actions:

1. Ask a friend to list their order of preferences for the same set of interests. Compare the lists.

2. Put your list away. One month later, and every New Year's Eve after, write down your current prioritized order. Compare that most recent list with your first one.

During either experiment, you will most likely see some differences between the two lists. This result occurs because different situations have directed us and our friends to our present positions in life, and our different interests will influence where we wish to go next. The differences between people—or even between ourselves during different time periods—suggest that learning principles, and not specific techniques for specific situations, will be more useful for our life's journeys.

Similarly, since our priorities may change throughout our lifetime, we must be cautious about lazily using the same rules that worked in our past, such as:

"Never kiss on the first date."
"Always save 10 percent of your paycheck."
"Birthday celebrations can only occur on your birthday."

Such rules may not be good guides for your current position in life. For example, imagine that one of your friends is getting married and has invited you to stand in the wedding party. However, the cost of the garments and the gift, as well as the travel expenses, would be substantial. If you always follow the rule "Live within your budget," then you may not be able to go to the wedding. Rigidly following this type of rule can unnecessarily constrain you. Alternatively, learning principle-centered intelligence will allow you to harmoniously integrate *Life's* competing priorities. For example, you may choose to exceed your <u>monthly</u> budget by attending the wedding and then live more frugally within the rest of your <u>yearly</u> budget (more on leveraging money and time later).

Uncovering Principles and Controls

The first principle guiding an understanding of our controls should be the concept of *growth*. Growth is necessary in order to counteract *entropy*, the principle that all things break down over time. Entropy occurs when we stop practicing a skill—that talent becomes rusty. Entropy occurs when we stop exercising—our muscles weaken. Entropy occurs when we stop changing the oil in our cars—the cars quit working. Entropy always occurs. No "thing," including ourselves, can ever stay the same. Thus, we either need to grow our *Life* controls and options, or we must accept that, over time, we will become weaker and our available alternatives for a happy life will decrease.

We grow our controls—or lose them—from the four common *Choices* that we all encounter throughout our lives. These choices become available to most of us when we are teenagers. For example, imagine some of the issues that students must deal with during a week of school (a partial list follows). Now, as a contrast, imagine some of issues that a CEO of a company will face during a typical business week (that partial list is also shown next). At first glance, the two sets of issues seem rather different and distinct:

Common Student Issues	Typical CEO Issues
Using "hip" / "cool" words	Finances & Accounting
Dating	Product Quality
Homework Projects	Marketing & Advertising
Sports Competitions	Company Strategy
Friendships	Deadlines & Forecasts
Spending Habits	Operating Legally
Acquiring Cash	Hiring & Firing employees
Clothing Styles	Creating Alliances

Although these two sets of activities appear to be different on the surface, separating them into their core control categories reveals a common set of *Choices,* as Figure 1-1 shows below (the student issues are listed above the CEO issues).

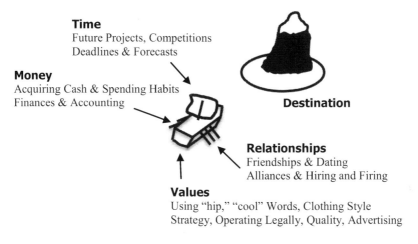

Time
Future Projects, Competitions
Deadlines & Forecasts

Money
Acquiring Cash & Spending Habits
Finances & Accounting

Destination

Relationships
Friendships & Dating
Alliances & Hiring and Firing

Values
Using "hip," "cool" Words, Clothing Style
Strategy, Operating Legally, Quality, Advertising

Figure 1-1: The Four Major Choice Controls

Figure 1-1 displays the four common *Choices* of *money, relationships, time,* and *values* that we use as we travel along our life's sea of possibilities. How well we develop our control of these categories affects our ability to reach our desired destinations. The four *Choices* work together, or against each other, as if they were the major components of a *Life-Altering* ship—a Greek trireme, in this case. The Greeks used this type of ship to defeat the Persians at the Battle of Salamis, around 480 BC. This battle also saved the Athenian practice of democracy (lucky for us!) and is recounted nicely in Barry Strauss's book, *The Battle at Salamis*.

A trireme used rowers as a power source for its travels. On our *Life* ship, the left set and right set of oars represent our most recognized sources of control—our money and relationships. Both sides need to work together in harmony for the ship to move forward. If they do not, then the boat struggles to advance. Consider what happens when one side rows with more force than the other. The imbalance causes the vessel to go in circles, as shown next in Figure 1-2:

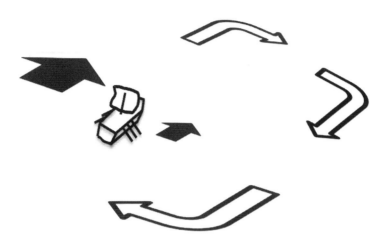

Figure 1-2: The Outcome of Unbalanced Control

This type of "effort that goes nowhere" can occur in people's daily lives. For example, consider what can happen if a man tries to present a wealthy, but false, first impression to a woman during their initial date. It is certainly noble that a man wants to treat a woman well, and wealth can help with part of his efforts. However, suppose that this man runs up credit card debt as he tries to impress his new romantic interest. Over time, as he continues spending well beyond his earnings, he will be sent "spinning" by the uneven balance between his money and his relationship. He may begin to suffer financial distress, as well as insecurity, as he realizes that his girlfriend might leave him if she discovers that he is not the image that he has created.

Eventually, he will need to admit his financial situation. She might understand. Alternatively, she might not appreciate that someone has tried to deceive her with a false image. She might interpret his confession as a sign that he is not honest unless he can no longer fake an image. If he had just been himself from the very beginning—instead of a "spinner"—both of their lives would have been saved from this unpleasant experience. By staying true to a balanced use of the four controls, people may avoid pursuing false happiness and the accompanying spinning.

Returning to our *Life* ship, our next potential power source for control comes from how we choose to use our time. Our interactions with time are similar to a ship's sail interacting with the wind. Many simple efforts

9

performed over time, which require relatively little energy, will result in long-term gusts of support that help us reach our goals. For example, one way to leverage our age and our expected years of life is by investing small amounts of our money every month. Over time, we can build up a sizable amount of money that will help us reach our desired goals. Alternatively, we may try to move against the "wind" by ignoring the benefits of time. Anyone who has ever tried to run or bike into the wind knows how rapidly an "against the wind" strategy depletes a person's energy and motivation. It is better to work with the wind rather than against it. We will see numerous examples of using time to our advantage as we explore the various *Life-Altering Choices*.

The final, and perhaps least obvious source of influence on our ship, is the steering of our lives by our values. Just as a boat's rudder is typically beyond the vision of an observer standing on the coast, our values are not immediately apparent to others when they first meet us. Sometimes, our values become revealed by our choices and our actions. If our values differ from someone else's, then that observer may look at one of our decisions and wonder, "How strange…why did they do that?!?" However, if the observers are close friends or family members who understand our values, then they will be able to more easily understand our decisions and what influenced them.

Developing a workable set of values and legal codes has been critical to history's great societies. Whether the religious guidance of Christian, Jewish, and Muslim values, or the governing codes of Roman, British, and American laws, a workable, guiding set of values has been associated with individuals and societies associated with growth and success. We will explore the various influences that impact our values—and our nation's values—in the pages ahead.

Growth + Focused Action = Destination

Did you notice how a "destination" island was located just beyond our *Life* ship on page 8? This is to remind us that our life should be filled with goals that we choose.

Why? Over two thousand years ago, a wise man named Confucius let his garden grow for an entire season, without tending to it once. He then invited his students to visit his home and see the results. When they arrived, the students could see only weeds where a harvest should have been.

Confucius used that moment to tell his students that a garden of potential, left unattended, would not produce fruit. Similarly, some people choose not to develop or understand their four control *choices*. They may even declare that they will live by "going with the flow." We must not succumb to this lazy attitude. The "flow" includes entropy, and it will reduce our chances at producing a life of fruitful results (more of Confucius's wisdom can be found in *The Analects of Confucius* by Simon Leys).

The results of an unfocused effort can be seen in many ways besides gardening. Consider what happens when a flashlight has its beam spread too wide—the resulting dim glow cannot light a path for us. However, if we tighten its focus, it becomes useful. Similarly, once we have chosen to develop our controls, we should focus them toward reaching goals and destinations. Otherwise, we may end up scattering our energy among so many priorities that we never accomplish any of them.

Although he did not use the specific ship of a Greek trireme for his explanations, C. S. Lewis, in his book *Mere Christianity*, also described our lives using ships. As a paraphrase of his words, C.S. Lewis wrote that it is not enough to simply keep our ship in good condition so that it stays afloat. We must also be certain that we do not crash into other ships and damage other people's lives. Additionally, we must have a destination for our ship. Otherwise, we could end up drifting our ship endlessly on the open seas, and never reach any destinations or achieve any goals.

Some people will never choose to focus their lives in pursuit of desired outcomes. Perhaps their lack of goals makes them feel safe because that approach reduces their chances of feeling disappointment or temporary failure. Perhaps they would rather just dream, and hope that someone else will come along and make their wishes come true. Such people never turn their dreams into realities because they never leave the dreaming state. We can do better than that.

As Stephen Covey wrote in his international best seller, *The 7 Habits of Highly Effective People*, the first habit of effective people is to "be proactive." This "*take action*" principle is a modern day continuation of Confucius's tale. Building upon that foundation, this book of *Life-Altering Choices* offers you explorations into the four major control choices where you should be proactive. No matter what you choose to do in *Life*, you will have to deal with money, relationship, time, and values. Not dealing with them is still a response, since entropy will always be impacting your status in *Life*. Rather than giving in to the challenging waves of entropy, you may choose to plot a course toward short-term and long-term goals. Even if you change your goals, you will benefit from your earlier efforts because you will have practiced an intelligent, principled pursuit of a destination. You need destinations. We will consider some potential destinations throughout this book, such as living a happier life by:

> 1) Becoming a millionaire by age 65, 55, or if really focused, 45.

> 2) Understanding the F.L.Y.—A.S.I.A. relationship factors of sexual attraction.

> 3) Evaluating whether a "zero percent" financing deal on a car is better for you than a $2,500 "cash back" offer.

Travelling with Companions

Navigating our finite lives across an infinite sea of options will require choosing from alternatives. This journey can be challenging and, at times, a struggle. You might consider whether you want to explore these trade-offs alone or with others (particularly others whose opinion you respect). Exploring your thoughts and ideas with another person, or in group discussions, offers you the advantages of multiple stories and viewpoints that may be exchanged, considered, and possibly debated (depending on your group's level of comfort).

Be careful if you choose to discuss ideas in groups that are larger than four or five members. As a group becomes larger, it becomes more difficult for you to be able to talk long enough to explain your ideas, as well as gain individually useful insights. At the extreme, if you try to educate yourself by seeking the opinions of the larger group known as "society," then the resulting, majority consensus would guide you toward achieving society's average outcomes, such as debt and divorce. We do not want to be "average." Small group discussions, whether about dating, family, or careers, often balances our views away from self-centered thinking while at the same time avoids the peer pressure of conforming to "what's popular with the big group."

If you are feeling a bit shy about sharing your personal beliefs with others, please feel free to use me or this book as the conversation opener. For example, you might begin a conversation with a lunchtime friend by saying, "So, I was reading this book by Dr. Maue (Mah-ow), and he believes that these five questions (at the end of a chapter) will help me find a better long-term relationship partner. What do you think?" Whether their responses completely agree, or only partially agree with your thoughts, such conversations will enrich your intelligence.

A Look Ahead

The journey before us has two major components. In the first part, each of the next four chapters will focus on one of the four major control *Choices*. At the same time, these chapters will follow the principle of being *holistic* by looking at the big picture of how each chapter's main *Choice* interacts with the other choices. Trying to discuss any one choice by itself is foolish. There were once four blind men who tried to guess what was in front of them. One felt the object and perceived a rope. Another felt the unknown object and thought that he had touched a fan. The third man was sure that he had found a spear, and the last man guessed a tree. What the four men actually felt were the tail, ear, tusk, and leg of an elephant. Their limited impressions left too much unknown. Similarly, having only a partial view of our choices in *Life* will leave us limited at first. However, when we understand all four parts of our *Life* ship, we shall plan our actions more intelligently. We will begin our *Life* exploration by looking at the very concrete and visible control of money, then move through the less quantifiable choices of relationships, time, and values.

The second part of this book will explore the daily challenges that we all encounter with decision-making, communication, and community interactions. Both parts of the book include reflection activities, as well as references to sources mentioned within each chapter. These resources will allow you to explore certain issues more deeply, should you so choose.

In keeping with the theme of this book—choices, not rules—remember that the references are only my suggestions. You could also use other sources to inform your opinions and reach your conclusions. If you look for these references at a bookstore website, consider exploring the list of "books like these" usually included with any book search. Similarly, if you visit a bookstore, consider glancing along the shelves beyond where your current interest is located… there may be similar books that you would find more useful for your journey.

*****

So far, we have categorized our *Life–Altering Choices* as money, relationships, time, and values. After acknowledging that there are not guaranteed steps to success, we began viewing the principles of growth, action, and holistic viewing as guides for our intelligent choices. These initial guides will stack the odds of success in our favor. We are now ready to begin a journey that will increase the strength, power, and control of our lives. Enjoy!

Principles:

Growth
Action
Holistic Viewing

For Further Reflection:

1) How did you prioritize the interests displayed on page 6? How did your priorities compare with your friends? What reasons do you believe caused the differences?

2) What are some of your goals that you would like to achieve in the next few years? What about by the time that you are age 40? 80?

For Further Investigation:

Marriage statistics referenced from: Bramlett MD and Mosher WD. *Cohabitation, Marriage, Divorce, and Remarriage in the United States*. National Center for Health Statistics. Vital Health Stat 23(22). 2002.

Debt statistics acquired from:
http://money.cnn.com/magazines/moneymag/money101/lesson9/

Jeff Hawkins, *On Intelligence*

Barry Strauss, *The Battle of Salamis*

Simon Leys, *Analects of Confucius*

C.S. Lewis, *Mere Christianity*

Stephen R. Covey, *The 7 Habits of Highly Effective People*

Money: Priority One (?)

"The most powerful force in the universe is compound interest."
                                                      – Albert Einstein

If you are currently undecided about what to achieve during your lifetime, then you might consider "become a millionaire" as your first priority. Journeying toward this destination will simultaneously increase your intelligence and your future life options.

Developing your intelligence begins by predicting how certain actions will lead to certain outcomes. With these predictions in mind, you may then plan to achieve an outcome and act out that plan. For example, suppose that you go to a store and see a batch of *Harry Potter* VCR tapes on sale as a clearance item ("no returns") for $10 apiece. You might predict that you could sell these tapes on eBay for $20. Motivated by your prediction, you spend $100 and buy 10 tapes. You go home and list your tapes on the web. Nobody buys a single tape. You feel disappointed, yet still you have gained something positive from the incident. What have you gained?

You have gained the chance to develop your intelligence by comparing the actual outcome of your endeavors with your original, predicted outcome. Since the actual result was different from your original prediction, you may review your prediction, planning, and action phases and attempt to uncover why the difference occurred. Sometimes, the difference occurs because you made an inaccurate assumption. In this example, perhaps the original prediction that the VCR tapes would sell for $20 was a bad assumption because nobody owns VCR players anymore. Alternatively, sometimes you make correct assumptions, but then an event beyond your control interferes with your process. Perhaps there actually were 25 VCR owners who would have each liked to have bought a new *Harry Potter* tape. Unfortunately, and previously unknown to you, another person had also been to that same store as you, bought 25 tapes, and then sold them on eBay for the cheaper price of $15 (and, of course, later paid the taxes on the profits).

Incorrect assumptions and outside interference can interrupt our achievement attempts, and sometimes it is difficult to uncover which factor (or factors) thwarted our efforts. This difficulty suggests that money might be the control most worthy of our initial focus. Compared to our other major *Life* control choices of relationships, time, and values, we can usually see the results of our money efforts the fastest, and usually with a greater understanding of what caused our success or failure. For example, the "he said, she said" dramas that surround the break ups of romantic couples are much more difficult to understand than knowledge about how saving a little extra money each month can make you wealthy. Focusing on money offers many rapid, principled, learning opportunities, which makes money a strong candidate for being the first control that we develop.

A less obvious reason for growing your money control first is that you can use it to support your other *Life* choices. Consider which of the following statements is more likely to be true:

(a) By focusing on building my money control first, I will increase my chances at romance.

(b) By focusing on building my romance control first, I will increase my chances at money.

Statement (a) appears to be the more likely sequence of events. By focusing on building your money control first, you increase your ability to meet more people through activities that inevitably require money, such as dinner dates, dancing at clubs, or weekend adventure groups. Money plays a part in almost any activity that we perform. Developing your money strength first will increase your future options.

Alternatively, developing a romance first may actually reduce your chances for growing money strength, partly because of the time and money costs of romance. Eventually, if properly formed, romantic couples can work together to grow their money strength, as we shall see. For the moment let us consider how you would gain much by developing your money strength first, if you do not have a burning desire to be in a relationship right now.

Caution and balance must be applied to any view that prioritizes money. Money is NOT our first *and only* goal. There is more to *Life* than becoming rich, and people's *Life* ships will suffer spinning effects if they focus only on money. These spinning effects have been experienced, or at least witnessed, by many people. As a result, these people started the rumor that "money is the root of all evil." Such a rumor seems believable because money can be connected to almost all activities that people engage in, and therefore money can easily be associated with almost all harmful activities. However, what is not included in this "money equals evil" rumor is that money can also be used to do good things. Just as a hammer can be used to build or demolish a house, money can be used to assemble or destroy lives. *People choose to act* with their money, for good or for greed, with regard to their relationships, time, and values. Regardless of whether you wish to amass a personal fortune or you want to pay for large, charitable deeds that help others, you will benefit from strengthening your money control.

If we fail to prioritize growing our money control, then the influence of entropy will reduce it. For example, suppose that in the year 1998 you placed $100 into a jar and buried it in the ground. In 1998, that $100 would have allowed you to purchase nearly 100 gallons of gasoline for your car. Ten years later, in the summer 2008, if you dug up the jar, that same $100 would not have been able to buy nearly as much gasoline—perhaps 30 gallons. Prices typically rise over time, causing our money to lose its strength. Rather than letting our money evaporate away like a puddle of water, we must direct our money to flow, like a river, toward larger future options.

Growing Our Money with Time

To demonstrate how "simple" it is to become a millionaire, the following money flow scenario has been created for you. To keep the calculations friendly, there are a few mathematically-kind assumptions about the growth of the money. More specifically, suppose that we could invest our money at a 10 percent annual interest rate. The impact of this 10 percent yearly growth, also known as a "return," can be calculated by the formula of:

Amount Invested + (Amount Invested x Percent Return) = End of Year Value

For example, if we invested $100 at the beginning of a year, with a 10 percent return, we would receive $110 at the end of the year:

Amount Invested	+	(Amount Invested	x	Percentage Return)	=	End of Year Value
$ 100	+	($100	x	10%)	=	
$ 100	+	($100	x	0.10)	=	
$ 100	+		$10		=	
					=	$110

On a larger scale, if we were able to invest $1000 for one year at a 10 percent interest rate, then the new value at the end of that year would be $1,100.

As Albert Einstein noted in the overview quote to this chapter, the compounding impact of our initial investment earning interest, plus our investment's interest earning interest, can be quite powerful after a period of years. To demonstrate this impact, let us compare the results of two different types of investors. These two different types of people wanted to become "millionaires" by the time that they retired. Having already taken actions to improve their investing intelligence, these graduates decided to save for their retirement years using the protections of an Individual Retirement Account ("I.R.A." for short). Since too many details about an I.R.A. would distract from the main point of this section, I will generalize for now and state that an I.R.A. fund is a great way to save for retirement because it allows your savings to grow tax-free. Some very user-friendly details about traditional and Roth I.R.A.s are available at investing websites such as *The Motley Fool* (www.fool.com) or in investment books such as *The Wall Street Journal Complete Personal Finance Guidebook* by Jeff Opdyke.

On the next pages, Tables 2-1 and 2-2 show the outcomes from two different "saving for retirement" strategies. Table 2-1 represents graduates who, starting with zero money saved, invested from ages 19-28 (10 years) at a 10 percent interest rate. At the beginning of each year, these "early savers" placed $2,000 into an Individual Retirement Account. In contrast, Table 2-2 shows the investment plan of those who waited until they were age 29 before they began saving. These "late savers" also saved $2,000 at the beginning of each year in an I.R.A. and earned a 10 percent return. The late savers attempted to make up for their late start by saving from ages 29-65 (37 years).

The calculations of Table 2-1 and Table 2-2 are:

(Start of Year Balance) = (Previous Year's End of Year Total)

+

(Amount Invested this Year)

...and...

(End of Year Total) = (Start of Year Balance) x (Interest Rate)

The results follow (with years 61-64 omitted to economize space):

Table 2-1 "Early Savers" (Invested $2,000 each year from ages 19-28)

Age	Amount Invested	Start of Year Balance	10% Interest	End of Year Total
19	$2,000	$2,000	$200	$2,200
20	$2,000	$4,200	$420	$4,620
21	$2,000	$6,620	$662	$7,282
22	$2,000	$9,282	$928	$10,210
23	$2,000	$12,210	$1,221	$13,431
24	$2,000	$15,431	$1,543	$16,974
25	$2,000	$18,974	$1,897	$20,872
26	$2,000	$22,872	$2,287	$25,159
27	$2,000	$27,159	$2,716	$29,875
28	$2,000	$31,875	$3,187	$35,062
29	$0	$35,062	$3,506	$38,569
30	$0	$38,569	$3,857	$42,425
31	$0	$42,425	$4,243	$46,668
32	$0	$46,668	$4,667	$51,335
33	$0	$51,335	$5,133	$56,468
34	$0	$56,468	$5,647	$62,115
35	$0	$62,115	$6,212	$68,327
36	$0	$68,327	$6,833	$75,159
37	$0	$75,159	$7,516	$82,675
38	$0	$82,675	$8,268	$90,943
39	$0	$90,943	$9,094	$100,037
40	$0	$100,037	$10,004	$110,041
41	$0	$110,041	$11,004	$121,045
42	$0	$121,045	$12,104	$133,149
43	$0	$133,149	$13,315	$146,464
44	$0	$146,464	$14,646	$161,110
45	$0	$161,110	$16,111	$177,222
46	$0	$177,222	$17,722	$194,944
47	$0	$194,944	$19,494	$214,438
48	$0	$214,438	$21,444	$235,882
49	$0	$235,882	$23,588	$259,470
50	$0	$259,470	$25,947	$285,417
51	$0	$285,417	$28,542	$313,959
52	$0	$313,959	$31,396	$345,355
53	$0	$345,355	$34,535	$379,890
54	$0	$379,890	$37,989	$417,879
55	$0	$417,879	$41,788	$459,667
56	$0	$459,667	$45,967	$505,634
57	$0	$505,634	$50,563	$556,197
58	$0	$556,197	$55,620	$611,817
59	$0	$611,817	$61,182	$672,998
60	$0	$672,998	$67,300	$740,298
65	$0	$1,083,871	$108,387	$1,192,258

Table 2-2   "Late Savers"   (Invested $2,000 each year from ages 29-65)

Age	Amount Invested	Start of Year Balance	10% Interest	End of Year Total
19	$0	$0	$0	$0
20	$0	$0	$0	$0
21	$0	$0	$0	$0
22	$0	$0	$0	$0
23	$0	$0	$0	$0
24	$0	$0	$0	$0
25	$0	$0	$0	$0
26	$0	$0	$0	$0
27	$0	$0	$0	$0
28	$0	$0	$0	$0
29	$2,000	$2,000	$200	$2,200
30	$2,000	$4,200	$420	$4,620
31	$2,000	$6,620	$662	$7,282
32	$2,000	$9,282	$928	$10,210
33	$2,000	$12,210	$1,221	$13,431
34	$2,000	$15,431	$1,543	$16,974
35	$2,000	$18,974	$1,897	$20,872
36	$2,000	$22,872	$2,287	$25,159
37	$2,000	$27,159	$2,716	$29,875
38	$2,000	$31,875	$3,187	$35,062
39	$2,000	$37,062	$3,706	$40,769
40	$2,000	$42,769	$4,277	$47,045
41	$2,000	$49,045	$4,905	$53,950
42	$2,000	$55,950	$5,595	$61,545
43	$2,000	$63,545	$6,354	$69,899
44	$2,000	$71,899	$7,190	$79,089
45	$2,000	$81,089	$8,109	$89,198
46	$2,000	$91,198	$9,120	$100,318
47	$2,000	$102,318	$10,232	$112,550
48	$2,000	$114,550	$11,455	$126,005
49	$2,000	$128,005	$12,800	$140,805
50	$2,000	$142,805	$14,281	$157,086
51	$2,000	$159,086	$15,909	$174,995
52	$2,000	$176,995	$17,699	$194,694
53	$2,000	$196,694	$19,669	$216,364
54	$2,000	$218,364	$21,836	$240,200
55	$2,000	$242,200	$24,220	$266,420
56	$2,000	$268,420	$26,842	$295,262
57	$2,000	$297,262	$29,726	$326,988
58	$2,000	$328,988	$32,899	$361,887
59	$2,000	$363,887	$36,389	$400,276
60	$2,000	$402,276	$40,228	$442,503
65	$2,000	$660,079	$66,008	$726,087

Look at the money position reached by the early savers who invested $2,000 each year when they were younger! They achieved the status of a millionaire by age 64. In contrast, the late savers ended up with *$400,000 less* than the early savers. Of course, the late savers were still able to grow their investments to an impressive *$720,000+*. Still, the compounding effect of interest over time left the early savers, who invested for 10 years, in a much stronger position than the late savers who had invested for 37 years. In fact, if the late savers wanted to achieve the same results as the early savers, then the late savers would have needed to save $3,284 (instead of $2,000) during each of their saving years.

High School and College Graduate "Opportunity Costs"

The previous example provides us insight about our *Life* choices and how the principle of *opportunity cost* affects us. An opportunity cost is a way of calculating the trade-offs of a choice. More specifically, an opportunity cost is the cost of NOT doing one choice because you have chosen to do something else. For example, if you choose (or have already chosen) to attend a traditional, four-year college, then you have most likely chosen to NOT work full-time at a job during that same time period and have therefore probably NOT saved anything in an I.R.A.. This time delay before saving in your I.R.A. costs you money!

If graduates are willing to work *and save* immediately after high school, most graduates could invest $2,000 into a tax-free retirement fund each year. Meanwhile, the students who choose a four-year or five-year college adventure often delay saving any money for retirement, sometimes until they are 28 or older. Graduates who choose to work full-time after high school, and start saving their money, gain the advantage of time magnifying all of the compound interest effects. In contrast, graduates who choose to attend college often pay an opportunity cost besides the initial cost of going to college—they pay the cost of not earning the wages from full-time work (and saving some of those wages). College seems more expensive when the view includes how college is an opportunity cost of saving.

This opportunity cost of college becomes even larger at the higher saving amounts. For example, at the time that this book was written, graduates could place up to $5000 every year into their I.R.A. accounts. If graduates saved their money using the same two methods that were demonstrated in

Table 2-1 and Table 2-2, but with the larger amounts of $3,000, $4,000, and $5,000, then the different results would be:

Yearly Savings	Early Savers	Late Savers	Late savers "catch up" Amount	Difference
$2,000	**$1,192,258**	**$726,087**	**$3,284**	**$1,284**
$3,000	$1,788,387	$1,089,130	$4,926	$1,926
$4,000	**$2,384,516**	**$1,452,174**	**$6,568**	**$2,568**
$5,000	$2,980,645	$1,815,217	$8,210	$3,210

Table 2-3: Age 65 Results at Higher Savings Levels

Table 2-3 above shows how the retirement savings of graduates can grow based upon their investing strategies. The row for the $2,000 Yearly Savings shows the end results of Table 2-1, as well as the "catch up" amount that the Late Savers would need to save each year in order to obtain the same retirement results as the Early Savers. As previously noted, late savers needed to save $3,284 instead of the $2,000 amount in order to achieve the same results. The difference between the two amounts was $1,284. The same calculations have been repeated for the yearly investment levels of $3,000, $4,000, and $5,000. Regardless of your choice to become an Early Saver or a Later Saver (or an early saver who goes to college!), the moral of the story is the same—compounding interest and time strengthen your money control.

To balance the view that college costs you the opportunity of becoming a millionaire, it should be noted that education beyond high school often leads to better paying jobs that help make up for the lost time. The U.S. Census Bureau has reported that workers "18 and over" with a bachelor's degree earn an average of $51,206 a year, while those with a high school diploma earn $27,915. It appears that, on average, college graduates should be able to afford the extra dollar amounts each year to make up for any lost savings time. Graduating from college appears to be financially worthwhile, even if you must acquire student loans (including from your parents) or perhaps work part-time and attend school at a slower pace (five years versus four). Regardless of what you choose (or chose), using financial measures are one way—but not the only way—to look at opportunity costs.

Earlier, in Chapter 1, we briefly explored how time was the wind to our *Life* ship, and that we would rather travel with the wind, versus against it. The act of saving money demonstrates how time boosts your strength. The earlier you start growing your money, the stronger your money power becomes. Now is the time to start growing! Becoming a millionaire is within your grasp—with or without college. The destination can be achieved without using any of the other three investment options that you control (more on those in a moment), or receiving any retirement funds from the Social Security Administration (for eligibility, visit www.ssa.gov).

(Incidentally, assuming a continued annual inflation rate of 2 to 3 percent, then over long periods of time, the future US stock market returns have been predicted to be approximately 6 percentage points better than inflation. Under these conditions (inflation could change), the long-term stock market "growth" has been projected to be approximately 8 to 9 percent. Table 2-1 used a higher estimate of 10 percent. If you would like to see the results of a more conservative, 6 percent calculation, and you do not wish to do all of your investment calculations by hand, you could buy a financial calculator with "time value of money" (TVM) functions to save you some time. Alternatively, *The Motley Fool* (www.fool.com) has some good short-cut calculators that analyze savings strategies for retirement, home mortgages, and other big financial decisions.)

We seek to grow our money...but to what size?

During high school, my friends and I first realized how very little money we had when we were working at our part-time jobs. We used to say:

I go to work to pay for the gas, insurance, and oil changes for my car…
…so that I can go to work.

Certainly there were times in the summer when we were able to work more hours and earn a lot of extra cash. However, during the school year we really noticed that we would need to change our current work outcomes if we wanted to achieve a better lifestyle. We needed to become financially wealthy. But what was "wealthy?" Did we need to save a million dollars? Did we need to wait until we were 60 or 70 years old before we could retire?

Being monetarily wealthy is a different concept to every person, yet it has a common essence. Wealthy people rarely go to work for their money—they are capable of living without needing to work at a "regular" job of 40+ hours per week. Although some wealthy people choose to work, they do not need to work because their money is already doing enough work for them. Stated another way, wealthy people often have investments that generate enough money to make traditional working unnecessary. Therefore, a *Life* destination worth considering is the wealthy goal of *living by using only the income that we receive from our investments*.

Once we achieve a wealthy status, we no longer have to live somewhere undesirable because our job demands it. We no longer need to keep buying work clothes, or pay for the commute to work. We also regain control over 8-10 hours of most of our days. Instead of having to work, we might enjoy using those hours in other ways such as working at interesting part-time jobs, performing uplifting charity work, or spending more time with our family and friends. Since becoming wealthy is so desirable, can we measure how close we are to this goal?

Your current progress toward being wealthy can be measured by the standard of living that you would have if you never worked at your job again. Many Americans are only able to maintain their standard of living because of the earnings from their jobs. One study by the Federal Reserve estimated that 43 percent of American families actually spend more than they earn and live at a higher standard of living than they should. Another estimate noted that if "average" Americans lost their jobs, then they would only be able to pay their current expenses for a month or two. These Americans are not pursuing the goal of becoming wealthy. Indeed, they would lose most of their money control if they were ever unemployed. Unlike those people, if we create income for ourselves in areas other than our jobs we will improve our odds of becoming wealthy.

There are at least four possible ways to reach the destination of wealthy. It is possible that you could use all four methods during your lifetime:

(1) Invest in another person, such as through marriage.
(2) Invest in physical assets, such as a business, real estate, or baseball cards.
(3) Invest in working for other people.
(4) Invest in paper assets, such as stocks, bonds, and mutual funds.

To improve our ability to achieve wealth, we will examine many of the rewards and risks associated with the last three processes. The first process of "marrying money" is, statistically speaking, highly unlikely and therefore worth little mention. At the same time, it should be noted (with some amusement) that a good dating life, if it leads to marriage, can be as profitable financially as an entire career as a worker, even if the marriage does not last. For example, when the former Beatle and rock legend Paul McCartney was divorced by his wife, the ex-wife received a divorce settlement worth millions of dollars. This is a rare example of how option (b) at the beginning of this chapter can be true!

The Rewards and Risks of Physical Investments

A slightly more realistic possibility for creating wealth is by starting your own business. Certainly, successful business people such as Bill Gates (Microsoft's co-founder) and Steve Jobs (Apple's co-founder) did quite well financially by investing their time, talents, and energy into their businesses. The book series *Rich Dad, Poor Dad* by Robert Kiyosaki offers many insights into the wealth producing opportunities of the business world. Alternatively, rather than starting your own business, you might consider investing in an established business franchise, such as Wendy's, Pizza Hut, or Panera Bread. Information on franchising opportunities is typically available at each company's website.

Another investment option is to work with an established business, such as Mary Kay Cosmetics, from "out of your home." These businesses can usually be started without needing to buy expensive buildings or paying large franchise fees. Many of the financial advantages associated with owning a business can be found in books such as *Own Your Own Corporation* by Garrett Sutton *et al*. Additional wealth insights, including how people become millionaires by owning businesses in less-than-obvious professions, can be found in *The Millionaire Next Door* by Thomas Stanley and William Danko.

Besides business ownership opportunities, creating wealth can also be pursued by investing in the physical objects of real estate properties. One interesting real estate investment method has been performed by some members of the military. I have met a number of military officers who bought a house near the military base where they served. When the officers needed to move their family to a new location, instead of selling their house, the moving officers would rent their house to other members of the community. Often, these community members were other military families who would only be living in the area for a year or two and did not want the hassle of buying, and later trying to sell, a home. As a result, I have known officers who have acquired over $1 million in properties while having other people pay for those properties via rent money. Such property investors receive income and tax-advantages that help grow their wealth. A beginning resource for such tax insights would be *Rich Dad's Real Estate Advantages* by Sharon Lechter and Garrett Sutton.

Aside from real estate and businesses, there remains an incredible variety of physical object investment options, including coins, artwork, and baseball cards. For example, there is one particular baseball card—the T206 John Peter "Honus" Wagner—that is sometimes referred to as the Mona Lisa of all trading cards. Known as "The Flying Dutchman," Wagner played the position of shortstop and was one of the first five inductees into Major League Baseball's Hall of Fame. It is believed that only 50 or so T206 Honus Wagner trading cards were ever produced. Some of these cards have sold for over $1,500,000. If the Wagner card holders ever sold their cards, then these sellers would be well on their way toward a wealthy status.

Of course, it would be odd to find an investment strategy that guaranteed wealth. Otherwise, everyone would be doing that strategy. People typically do not invest in physical objects because of the risk of losing the money that they invest. For example, it has been estimated that nearly half of all small businesses fail within their first five years. Such failures might severely harm our money strength, especially if starting a business had required using a large part of our own savings, or a loan from the bank.

Other investments offer you different kinds of risk. With real estate, it is possible that no one will want to buy, or rent, your property when you are ready to move to a new location. As a result, you may need to lower the selling or renting price that you originally asked. This rising and falling in real estate values can also occur with other physical objects. For example, it is possible that one day people will look at that "Flying Dutchman" card and simply think, "I do not think that any piece of cardboard can be worth more than $500,000." If everyone thought that, then some of the current Wagner card holders might lose $1,000,000 if they tried to sell their cards.

With so many possible circumstances affecting physical object investments, no one "expert" can perfectly predict which type of investment will grow the best. Yet because of the bias that people have for bragging about their personal good news, we will be exposed to many stories in our lifetime about the world's investment "geniuses" who, by careful research or dumb luck, were able to invest in ways that made their money grow fast and large. Much like the story of a lottery winner, good news travels fast, sometimes in the form of front-page headlines, television time, and book titles. However, we rarely see or hear about the thousands of people that lost their money attempting various investment strategies. We must remember that there are risks that precede any reward. The principle of *risking for reward* affects all investment strategies.

At the same time, we should analyze any fears of risk that prevent us from attempting one of these uncommon wealth-growing strategies. After all, we accept risks every time we drive a car, travel by plane, or even go for a walk. What, then, gives us a comfort level of "acceptable risk?" Once again, intelligence provides us an answer. Being familiar with a set of circumstances and gaining a reasonable ability to predict outcomes takes us closer to finding acceptable levels of risk. For example, our driving experiences have given us the ability to predict that driving at night when our car's lights do not work will most likely lead to a bad outcome, such as a crash. However, with working car lights, we are willing to accept the risks associated with driving at night. There will always be risks. We just need find ways to reduce those risks down to acceptable levels.

Therefore, if we can become more familiar with investing in physical assets, then we will reduce the chances of investing in assets that result in us losing all of our money. For example, renting a house is less risky if that house is in good condition and close to a university or a military base, because these types of communities are more likely to have a large population of people who will only live in the area for a few years. Temporary dwellers often prefer to rent, instead of buy, their living space. Is this one piece of information enough to make real estate investing an "acceptable risk?" For most of us, probably not. However, we could reduce the risk further by acquiring additional intelligence about property through books such as *Rich Dad's Advisors: The ABC's of Real Estate Investing*, by Ken McElroy.

Seeking out such books, websites, and other investment professionals will give you greater knowledge and familiarity with investing so that you may improve your ability to reduce risk. This is why I have included some of my previous sources of learning at the end of each chapter. Of course, I have included mine only as a *suggested* starting point. There are often other information products similar to the ones I have referenced. You know yourself better than I do. Research your options, choose what you think will help you, and learn from the results.

The Rewards and Risks of Working for Others

Another investment possibility for creating wealth occurs when you work at a traditional job. While we do not wish to make our job our *only* source of earnings, our jobs can be leveraged into additional sources of income that will increase our options in life. For example, suppose that you choose to pursue the goal of "become wealthy enough to retire." Some graduates can reach this goal by working extra hours at their current job, or a second job, and saving the extra money. Other graduates acquire a portion of their retirement wealth by choosing careers that offer them income from an early retirement pension.

As a rather unique example, consider the retirement system of the United States military. It pays a retirement pension to its members after they have served for 20 or more years. When people join the military as officers and perform well, they might achieve the rank of Lieutenant Colonel during their 20 years of service. When these Lieutenant Colonels with 20 years of service retire (typically as 42 year-olds), they receive an annual pension of around $43,000 (before taxes) a year for the rest of their lives (with yearly adjustments for inflation). Mathematically speaking, this is similar to becoming a millionaire who has placed a million dollars in a bank receives a guaranteed yearly income from an interest rate of 4.3 percent on that untouched amount ($1,000,000 x 4.3% = $43,000). This is a bit of a generalization—the taxes associated with interest income often differ from job income taxes. Still, this type of pension will provide income to the "retired" individuals for the rest of their lives. This type of guaranteed income would take many of us closer to our goal of becoming wealthy—living from money that does not come from us working at a job every day.

This "military millionaire" story is not designed to make you want to join the military. Indeed, people who are only motivated by money, instead of by a desire to serve America's ideals, will have a hard time handling the conditions that deployed military members experience when they are in life-threatening combat zones. A military career requires that its members give up civilian opportunities and freedoms for 20 or more years and live within unique military standards, such as an annual physical fitness test. Additionally, if a person leaves the active-duty military before serving for 20 full years, then that person receives no retirement pension benefits (there are always some exceptions, such as for certain military reservist programs). The "military millionaire" scenario is presented only to highlight how productive efforts in certain careers may bring about additional sources of income. At the same time, if you are interested in joining the Air Force, Army, Navy, Marines, or Coast Guard, then information about these forces can be found at: www.airforce.com, www.goarmy.com, www.navy.com, www.marines.com, and www.gocoastguard.com.

No matter where you choose to work after graduation, you will want to consider an interesting point about working for others—hard work alone will not make you wealthy. Normally, we do not get paid what we are worth. Instead, we get paid according to what *our job* is worth. Job wages are often based on the job's working conditions, knowledge requirements, and the job's level of impact to its organization and its customers. Therefore, working hard in some jobs will not earn us as much money as working hard in more impacting jobs. For example, you could be the fastest, most polite and efficient grocery bagger in an entire store. Yet even if you worked diligently for 70 hours every week, you would probably not become as wealthy as the manager of that store.

Here is a thought experiment: If you ever wonder why someone is earning a certain pay rate, ask yourself one simple question: "How hard is it to replace this person?" If it seems relatively easy to be replace that person, then the wages that they receive are probably low. For example, I used to work at a restaurant as the "fry guy" who deep-fried chicken nuggets and potatoes. To be trained for that job, I watched a 20-minute video and was supervised by an experienced fryer for the first hour. After that, I was on my own...and I was easily replaceable. I earned a little more than minimum wage.

Generally speaking, unskilled physical labor is easy to replace, and it is becoming even easier to replace. As the nations of the world continue to move toward becoming one global economy, unskilled workers have become available in nations such as China and Mexico at rates that are much cheaper than in the United States. For this reason, many companies choose to build their products in these foreign countries and then pay for the shipment of the products to America. Even with the extra shipping costs, these companies are often able to sell their products at a cheaper rate than the comparable "made in the USA" products. With so many international sources of reliable, low-skilled labor, it is risky for graduates to choose a physical assembly job for their earnings. Unskilled labor sources within the United States are already plentiful because of high school graduates and immigrants who do not acquire specific job skills. Whether the labor competition comes from the people down the street or the people across the border, the ability to easily replace a low-skilled worker influences physical labor wages to be relatively low. More information on the labor effects from the global economy can be found in books such as *The World is Flat* by Thomas Friedman.

At the other end of the skills spectrum, when it is difficult to replace a person, the job earnings are usually higher. For example, it is a bit challenging to find a good college business professor who has a minimum of 20 years of educational experiences (e.g., K-12, 4-year undergraduate, probably 2 years for an M.B.A. or other Master's degree, as well as 4-5 years for a business Ph.D.). Business professors are even harder to find because people with a business interest usually stop their education at the M.B.A. level and pursue business wealth. The resulting small supply of graduates from good business Ph.D. programs makes it hard to replace "b-school" professors, and thus good b-school professors earn more than $110,000 in pay during their first year and can eventually earn more than $200,000 a year in their jobs.

As an extreme example of highly skilled individuals that are in small supply, consider professional athletes. Players such as Tiger Woods, Annika Sorenstam, Alex Rodriguez, Peyton Manning, Maria Sharapova, and LeBron James demonstrate how to earn millions of dollars each year by possessing talents that are in low supply, highly demanded, and not easily duplicated by others.

Of course, high earning workers faced many opportunity costs before receiving their big pay. Whether as an athlete, a technology inventor, or a business genius, these "best at their job" experts usually began their journey toward excellence by sacrificing large portions of their leisure time, relationships, and (initially, at least) money so that they could focus on developing their skills. As a result, they have been able to compete well in their high intensity jobs.

To qualify for such high intensity jobs, you will most likely need to follow the principle of developing strong *core competencies*. Core competencies are things that you do better than anybody else. In the business world, Walmart has been extremely successful because it has a core competency of being able to provide customers products at a low price. At the same time, Porsche has been successful by selling high priced, high quality, sports cars. Each company has different core competencies, yet each has been successful.

What are your core competencies? Take a look at your friends, and those who are not your friends. What is different between you and them? Maybe you have a talent, such as singing, that you do better than most people. Maybe you have an interest, such as playing video games, that is a stronger passion for you than most people. If you take time to look at your choices of the past and your current interests, then you might be able to uncover what you naturally gravitate toward. These natural tendencies could be developed into your core competencies, making you the next *American Idol* or the next software development millionaire. We will return to the principle of core competencies at the end of this chapter and throughout the rest of this book.

Once again, we must mention the principle of *risk for reward* when it comes to investing in your "uniqueness." Imagine a scenario where you wanted to be so good, so irreplaceable, and so unique that you only developed one skill. For example, pretend that you wanted to be a professional athlete so bad, that you did very little studying in high school. Instead, you were disciplined and spent every possible moment developing your speed, strength, and reflexes. You chose to gamble that being extremely good at one thing—athletics—would make you better than anyone else who would try out for the college level. Suddenly, during your senior year of high school, you suffer an injury, and it takes away your athletic ability. With no other abilities developed, you suddenly find yourself below everybody else's skill level at everything. You are no longer competitive for a university sports team, and you are not competitive academically. What would you do?

Dwayne Johnson was pursuing his goal (but not his only goal) of becoming a professional football athlete when he suffered a major injury during college. Rather than crumbling from how the injury reduced his "football athletics" skill to below average, he worked to develop himself into the "athletic entertainer" known as "The Rock" in the WWE sports entertainment industry. Towering at over 6 foot 5 inches, 270 pounds, "The Rock" combined athleticism, personality, and discipline to do truly irreplaceable things. He then developed himself into an "entertainer who is athletic," performing on Saturday Night Live and starring in numerous big screen films. Dwayne was able to recover from the risk and reality of injury because he had developed more than one core competency. Dwayne's autobiographical book (up through his WWE days in the year 2000) is *The Rock Says*, co-authored by himself and Joe Layden.

Most of us will choose to not pursue a professional sports career. We will still have risks associated with our jobs. Our company could go bankrupt, for reasons ranging from low customer sales to company corruption. Alternatively, new employees could be hired to do our jobs at a cheaper rate. Thus, it is risky to see yourself only as "an employee of organization X." Instead, consider seeing yourself as someone who works for organization X "right now." If that job were to disappear, what core competencies do you possess that would earn you a next job? You might find that the skills that would make you more competitive for jobs at other companies will also make you more irreplaceable within your own company.

The preceding discussion about pursuing high paying, high intensity jobs assumed that such jobs were more desirable than lower paying jobs. High intensity jobs are not necessarily more desirable. For example, when some "40 hours per week" workers leave their jobs for the day, they may leave their job stress at the workplace. In contrast, more than a few successful engineers and managers usually worked "half days" for some period of their career—6 a.m. until 6 p.m—as well as continued thinking about work after dinner. Business concerns, such as improving product quality and taking care of employees, continually challenged their minds. Similarly, skilled workers such as doctors and mechanics must stay "current" and at the cutting edge of their profession. They must invest part of their time toward *not* earning money, and instead attend training conferences to remain current with the latest techniques and technologies. Their high impact jobs typically include long hours, travel away from friends and family, and greater demands from deadlines and training requirements. Only you can decide if these opportunity costs are worth the higher earnings. These choices reflect the interactive nature of money, relationships, time, and values.

You might also choose to prioritize other factors besides the money that you could earn from your job. If you only focus on the job's annual pay, pensions, or health benefits, you may end up in a high paying job that you despise. Non-money factors such as interesting work and training opportunities, a fun group of coworkers, convenient work hours, and a great work location can make lesser paying jobs more desirable. We will investigate these trade-offs in more detail as we continue our *Life* journey.

Ultimately, you improve your chances of finding a great job by building up your skills, and making yourself "difficult to replace." Formal education, prior jobs, and interesting work-related experiences such as internships and studying abroad are ways enhance your intelligence and make you more valuable to companies with high impact jobs. To better predict the skills that will be highly valued in the jobs that you most desire, consider exploring websites such as www.monster.com, www.careerbuilder.com, or www.usajobs.com to learn what skills and job qualifications are most likely to be appreciated. You might also consider going to various website search engines, such as the one within www.Forbes.com, and search with phrases such as "high demand career" to discover what skills are currently highly desired.

The Rewards and Risks of Investing in Paper Assets

Since we want to strengthen our monetary income with more than just our jobs, we might consider investing in paper assets. Much like our dollar bills, these paper assets represent ownership of some value. For example, you can choose to invest in a specific company and receive shares of stock in return (which are written on paper). This makes you a "share holder." If one of your companies earns a profit and shares the profits with its shareholders, then you as a shareholder will receive income in the form of a dividend check. You may choose to cash in the dividend, or re-invest the dividend back into the company. You also have the right to sell your shares of that company.

Such paper assets can usually be traded for their current cash value within a day. For that reason, most paper assets are said to be "liquid" because they are able to easily flow from their paper asset form into cash for you. In contrast, if you buy a piece of property, or art, or a business, it is possible that someone may not want to buy it from you right away. The low liquidity aspect of these types of investments can be troubling if you need to rapidly acquire money.

As with all investments, there is some risk with investing in paper assets. With paper assets, the biggest risk is that the price of your shares may go down after you first buy them. The business history of the Enron company exemplifies how extremely, and possibly dangerously, risky it is to place all of your investments into just one company. In less than a year, Enron's stock price went from a value of $90 to being worth $42, and six months later it was worth only pennies. Billions of dollars were lost by investors, and thousands of jobs were lost by Enron employees as the company went bankrupt. For a brief synopsis of the Enron scandal, see http://en.wikipedia.org/wiki/Enron, or see the movie *Enron: The Smartest Guys in the Room,* to gain a fuller appreciation of how greed, corruption, and risk brought financial pain to thousands of American employees and investors.

How then, do we manage the risk of investing in paper assets down to an acceptable level ("no risk" is not really an option)? The two most important prediction tools that we have at our disposal are diversity and time. Let us investigate the use of diversity first.

We use the tool of diversity to ensure that we invest our money in multiple companies. Yet diversity is more than investing "money in a multiple companies." For example, if we invest in Dell, Apple, Intel, and Microsoft, then we have not really diversified our investment because we have been investing in the general category of computer technologies. Investing in many companies within one category is less risky than investing in just one company, but it still has more risk than necessary. The additional risk of computer technologies would become apparent if customers stopped buying new computers for a full year—the value of most computer technology companies would simultaneously start to fall, and then the value of your company shares would drop as well. When you truly diversify, you need to buy shares of stock from numerous business categories such as retail (Walmart), communications (Verizon), automotive (Ford), and food (Wendy's…as usual, these are not "official recommendations"). It would take large amounts of money to buy enough stocks to make us well diversified investors. Fortunately, there is a way to buy shares in hundreds of companies for very little money each month. The answer is a diversified "mutual fund."

A mutual fund is a way for people to mutually combine their money together, usually through an investment firm such as Vanguard or USAA. The investment firm uses the combined pool of money from investors to buy shares of various company stocks. One type of mutual fund that nearly all investment firms offer is a Standard and Poor's 500 fund, or "S&P 500" for short. These S&P 500 funds invest the collected money in many of the 500 largest companies in America.

A 10-year pattern of risk and reward for an S&P 500 fund could look something like Chart 2-4:

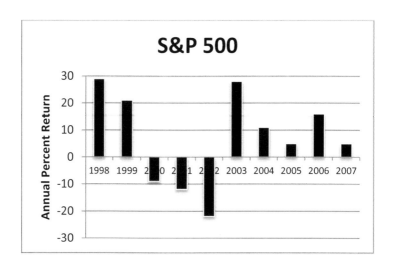

Chart 2-4: Potential 10-year returns of a typical S&P 500 fund.

Chart 2-4 shows the typical returns for S&P 500 funds during the years 1998-2007. Although more recent information could be used, this time period is particularly useful because it illustrates the *risk for reward* principle. If you had invested money in an S&P 500 fund in the beginning of 1998, that investment would have been nearly 30 percent larger at the end of the year. Thus, $10,000 invested on January 1, 1998, would have been worth $13,000 if you had sold it at the end of the year. This is much better than the 10 percent return that we assumed during the "retirement I.R.A. scenario" near the beginning of this chapter.

At the same time, can you see where the risk of losing money became a reality? The years 2000-2002 were years of loss for S&P 500 investors. Money that was invested at the beginning of 2002 in a typical S&P 500 fund lost around 20 percent of its value. During that year, a $10,000 investment shrunk to a value of only $8,000. Of course, you only would have suffered a loss if you had sold your investment at the end of that year. If you were able to hold on to your shares for a few more years, your value would have recovered to above the $10,000 amount. The S&P 500 example demonstrates how even a diversified investment across 500 companies can be risky, especially when impacted by a slower economy and the fallout from a business scandal, such as the Enron meltdown years of 2000-2002. The year 2008, with its numerous financial institution collapses, was also a major loss year for the broad market of S&P type investments—many S&P funds lost 30% of their worth in one year!

Fortunately, we noted that there were two tools for reducing risk—not just diversity, but also time. If we were to look at Chart 2-4 across the full 10 years, we would notice that $10,000 invested in 1998, even after going through the negative years of 2000-2002, would have earned the equivalent of an annual return of about 6 percent each year and would have been worth around $17,700 at the end of 2007. Using time as a critical ally, investors who could hold on to their S&P 500 investment avoided the major loss and then benefited from a return in economic growth. That is why many people perform a "buy and hold" strategy with their stock market investments—they buy an S&P 500 mutual fund and hold on to it for a long period of time. Such a "buy and hold" strategy makes a lot of sense when you are ready to start saving for your retirement using your I.R.A. privilege of tax-protected growth. The downside to an I.R.A. protected investment is that you can usually only begin withdrawing money from your I.R.A. once your reach your 60s. There are always exceptions to the rules, as noted before, and more information on I.R.A.s can be found at www.fool.com and www.guidedchoice.com.

In addition to holding stocks for longer time periods, another way to reduce your risks is to diversify in mutual funds that use categories other than stocks. For example, most investment firms offer some kind of mutual fund that is composed of treasury bonds, bank certificates, and mortgage contracts. These types of investments are typically less risky than buying shares of a company's stock. Such a mutual fund typically has the word "Income" in its title. One possible pattern of an Income fund would be Chart 2-5:

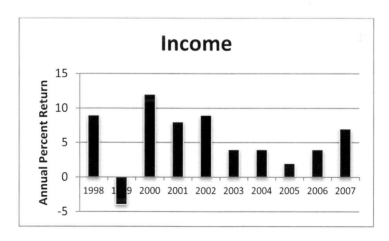

Chart 2-5: Potential 10-year returns of a typical Income fund.

Chart 2-5 shows the return rates of an Income fund during the years 1998-2007. With this type of fund, if you had invested $10,000 at the beginning of 1998, it would have been worth around $10,900 at the end of the year, due to the 9 percent return. For any given year, when an S&P 500 fund is returning positive income, an Income fund's less risky assets are usually returning a positive value as well, but it will usually be a smaller percent.

At the same time, Chart 2-5 shows a major benefit of investing in the less risky Income fund. There was only one year when the Income fund lost money, and that was a meager four percent. Compared to the years when the S&P 500 fund lost value, the Income fund lost less, or even returned a positive gain. In fact, this Income fund returned positive income during the years 2000-2002, which were years of loss for S&P 500 investors. Overall, $10,000 invested in the Income fund in 1998 would have earned the equivalent of an average interest rate of about 5.5 percent, and would have been worth approximately $16,900 at the end of the decade. Since it is a less risky asset category, Income funds generally, over the long term, produce lower returns than an S&P 500 fund.

However, not all risk-reducing strategies reduce the potential rewards. Consider what would have happened if you had invested 50 percent of your $10,000 in 1998 in an S&P 500 fund and the other 50 percent in an Income fund. Your yearly returns for that same period might have then looked like Chart 2-6:

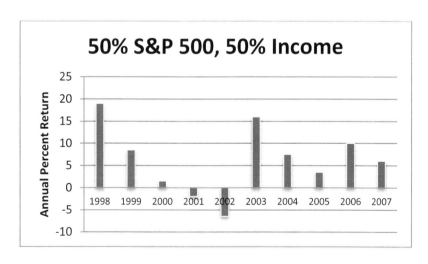

Chart 2-6: Potential 10-year returns of an evenly allocated investment in S&P 500 and Income Funds.

Chart 2-6 shows the annual returns from investing half of your money in a typical S&P 500 and the other half in a typical Income Fund. With diversity and time, this new allocation of investments achieved a slightly higher rate of return than investing in the S&P 500 alone. $10,000 invested in 1998 would be worth approximately $18,100 under these conditions. This higher return was achieved without having dramatic losses or gains like the S&P 500. Of course, there are no guarantees that combining these types of funds will always increase your earnings. However, there is a pretty large set of evidence that a well diversified set of investments reduces your risk of a major loss.

Beyond the previous simplified examples, there are numerous categories of mutual funds available for achieving investment diversity. For example, if you do not want to buy just one piece of real estate, then you might consider investing in a Real Estate Investment Trust (REIT) mutual fund that invests the collected pool of money into multiple properties, from golf courses to beach houses. You might also consider investing outside of the category of American businesses by investing part of your money in a mutual fund of Europe, Asia, and Far East investments (EAFE funds). Your choice of asset classes should be taken seriously—researchers, such Nobel Laureate William Sharpe, have shown that nearly 90 percent of the difference in the returns that investors earn can be linked to the type of funds and asset classes in which they invested.

With so many options available, it can initially seem overwhelming to invest in paper assets. Yet there is a reason to have courage. An impressive prediction about what could happen to our money in paper assets has been written by Burton Malkiel within his book, *A Random Walk Down Wall Street*. "Impressive" is not a word to be used lightly, and I dare to use it because his book has been updated and re-released multiple times during the last 20 years. Its reader-friendly stories, risk reducing statistics, and evidence supporting the benefits of an S&P 500 mutual fund make it a "must read" for improving your investment intelligence!

Time Horizon Targeting

One other timing issue that you should consider when saving your money is your investment "horizon." Your horizon is the amount of time until you need to convert your investment back into cash so that you may purchase something. You use your investment horizons to guide your choice of investments. For example, suppose that you wanted to save for a down payment on a big house that you would buy in 10 years. To keep this example manageable, pretend that you could only invest in two types of assets—the S&P 500 index fund, with its riskier and higher long-term returns, and the less risky, but lower returning, Income fund.

Timeline 2-7 shows an investment horizon plan that you might consider using:

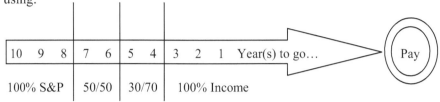

Timeline 2-7: Simplified 10-year Investment Horizon Example

With a 10-year horizon, you might consider initially saving for your house down payment by using the riskier investment of an S&P 500 fund. You would do this with the hope that you will have a year or two of strong gains. Alternatively, if the S&P fund goes down in value, there are still a number of years left for the fund to go up in value, like it did after the year 2002.

As you get closer to your goal, you will most likely want to reduce your risk of having a year of big losses. Therefore, at the six-year horizon, you might consider taking out half of your S&P 500 value and placing that half in a safer investment, such as an Income fund. Any new money that you invest should probably also go toward the 50/50 allocation (50 percent to the S&P 500 fund, 50 percent to the Income fund). If you want even less risk of losing money (and most likely lower gains), then you should save any new money for the house in the Income fund.

The process of reducing the risk of a big loss continues at the four-year horizon, with a reallocation of funds so that no more than 30 percent of your total house savings is now in an S&P 500 fund. During the final years, you would most likely shift all of your money over to an Income fund because you do not want to risk a serious loss in the overall value of your saved money.

Of course, your own tolerance of risk will most likely lead you to different percent allocations than the above horizon timeline. The concept of allocating your money to match your goals will be further developed in the upcoming *Time* chapter.

*****

In this chapter, we have focused heavily on developing control of your *Life* journeys through your choices with money, because it might be your first priority. We have also uncovered the principles of opportunity cost, risking for reward, and core competencies. While it is a good start to understanding your *Life* ship, it is not enough.

We have yet to consider how much of our money we should invest so that we may retire as wealthy people. We have yet to choose what kind of person might be worthy of sharing our wealth. Indeed, we have yet to decide if we want to be wealthy. Such decisions will be further explored in the upcoming chapters. For now, we continue by exploring the interactions of money, values, and time with the other side of our rowing strength, and our next chapter—*Relationships*.

Additional Principles:

Risk for Reward
Opportunity Cost
Core Competency

For Further Reflection:

1) What does "wealthy" mean to you? What would your ideal standard of living be? What about your friends? Is their standard of living the same? Why do you differ?

2) How much risk are you willing to take with your investments? Consider going to a website such as www.vanguard.com, and look at their different mutual funds. Which ones offer the most risk? The most reward / highest returns? The least risk? What is common about the riskier mutual funds? What is common about the safer mutual funds?

3) Write down three things that you do better than 80% of your peers (friends or "average" strangers). Some of these potential core competencies might be:

- the ability to learn material quickly
- the ability to learn hands-on tasks quickly
- the ability to bring humor to a situation
- the ability to be athletic
- the ability to win competitive games
- the ability to be trusted with a secret
- the ability to be a non-judgmental listener
- the ability to remain calm
- the ability to be persistent
- the ability to sing, paint, or decorate

4) What might be the dream job for someone with your set of core competencies? Alternatively, what kind of business would you like to manage? What skills do you think you will need? How much travel, time away from home/family, hours of long work, etc., are you willing to accept?

5) What is your dream job (relative to working for someone else)? Consider going to www.monster.com, www.careerbuilder.com, or www.usajobs.com and seeing what the qualifications are for such a job. Alternatively, ask a job counselor, career counselor, academic advisor, or someone who works at a location where you would want to work about job qualifications. Do you wish to commit the energy to acquire the necessary rare skills?

For Further Investigation:

The Motley Fool, www.fool.com

Jeff Opdyke, *The Wall Street Journal Complete Personal Finance Guidebook*

Census Bureau data from: Mike Bergman. "College Degree Nearly Doubles Annual Earnings, Census Bureau Reports," http://www.census.gov / Press-Release / www / releases / archives / education /004214.html

The Social Security Administration, www.ssa.gov

43% spend more than they make, from Kim Kahn's "How does your debt compare?" http://moneycentral.msn.com/ content / Saving and Debt / P70741.asp

Average American saves less than 1 month's expenses, from David Bach's "Make Your Emergency Savings Automatic," http:// finance .yahoo. com / expert / article / millionaire / 8933

http://www.hollywood.com/news/McCartney_to_Give_Mills_A_235_Mi llion_Divorce_Package/3597152   By WENN | Sunday, December 10, 2006

Robert T. Kiyosaki, *Rich Dad, Poor Dad*

Thomas J. Stanley and William D. Danko, *The Millionaire Next Door*

Garrett Sutton, Robert T. Kiyosaki, and Ann Blackman, *Own Your Own Corporation*

Sharon L. Lechter and Garrett Sutton, *Rich Dad's Real Estate Advantages*

Ken McElroy, *Rich Dad's Advisors: The ABC's of Real Estate Investing*

Thomas Friedman, *The World is Flat*

Military Pay Tables available at: http://www.dfas.mil/militarypay/militarypaytables/2008MilitaryPayChart.pdf

The Military Websites: www.airforce.com, www.goarmy.com, www.navy.com, www.marines.com, and www.gocoastguard.com.

Hard work analogies can also be found in *Winning through Intimidation* by Robert J. Ringer

The Rock and Joe Layden, *The Rock Says*

44

www.monster.com

www.careerbuilder.com

www.usajobs.com

www.Forbes.com

Enron: The Smartest Guys in the Room.

www.guidedchoice.com

More investment insight on mutual funds and their associated risks and rewards can be found at www.vanguard.com and www.usaa.com

William Sharpe, "Asset Allocation: Management Style and Performance Measurement: An Asset class factor model can help make order out of chaos," *Journal of Portfolio Management,* Winter 1992.

Relationships: Overcoming the FLY—ASIA Influences

A chain is only as strong as its weakest link. – Machiavelli

People are more likely to die without good relationships. Studies have shown that, compared to people who are surrounded by positive relationships, people who <u>lack</u> a solid support mechanism—such as a spouse, family, or community—are more likely to die when they encounter various harsh challenges. It also appears that the supportive relationships do not even have to be human in nature. For example, studies have shown that pet owners are more than twice as likely to live for a year after a heart attack than non-pet owners. Ongoing research has also discovered that, by the time people reach their 50s, if they are able to answer that they have lived a life that involved good people, then they are more likely to be healthier in their 80s than other 50 year-olds who cannot say that they have interacted with good people. Reader-friendly versions of these types of studies can be found in books such as *Aging Well* by George Valliant and *Love & Survival* by Dean Ornish.

With so many benefits coming from good relationships, you might be inclined to think that people would develop their relationship intelligence so that they could build positive, lasting relationships. However, the facts suggest otherwise. For example, consider how well people choose their marriage partners. Approximately half of the people who marry for the first time end up divorcing. After they become divorced, some of these people choose to remarry. We might expect that these "divorced once" people would have learned from their first attempt at marriage and not repeat their earlier mistakes. Once again, the facts suggest otherwise. Of those who divorce and remarry, nearly 50 percent of these people end up divorcing again.

To help avoid a similar fate, we will build up our predictive relationship abilities during this chapter. Much like money, relationships impact our power to achieve our goals in visible ways. Each relationship connection that we make is like an investment—each friendship, romance, or work group bond that we create requires an initial contribution on our part. Yet each contribution does not necessarily result in a positive return for us. Some relationship investments simply drain our energy. When a relationship turns extremely bad, such as when a marriage breaks down and ends in divorce, it can send a person's *Life* ship spinning.

As they did with money, the principles of *risking for reward* and *opportunity cost* also accompany our understanding of relationships. For example, compared to people who are married, single people have more opportunities to pursue personal and professional interests. As we saw in the *Money* chapter, the development of job skills and potential was almost completely under each graduate's control. However, this assumed that the graduate was not in a significant relationship. Once you enter into a committed relationship, you give away some of your control. Since your choices will impact your partner, and your partner's choices will impact you, it would be self-centered if either of you made decisions by considering only what you alone wanted. The career choices that are best for you as an individual may not be the choices that are best for your relationship. As a result, it seems likely that you will choose differently when you are in a committed relationship, versus when you are single, if you value your relationship more than your career.

Those graduates who are single and not involved in a romantic relationship may not experience all of the extra highs that come from a good relationship, but they certainly avoid the lows that come from a poor relationship. Indeed, people who enter into poor relationships may fare worse than if they had remained single. Improving our *ability to accurately predict* who we should connect our life with, and who we should detach from, will help reduce our relationship risks and opportunity costs down to manageable levels.

Reducing our costs and risks with these choices poses a unique challenge. Ordinarily, if we want to become better at something, we need to practice that something…a lot. This applies to a variety of activities, ranging from practicing a sport with a team to practicing with a musical instrument as an individual. During these types of practices, we often make mistakes. Fortunately, when we make those mistakes, the overall impact is usually quite small. Musical instruments and sports equipment have no memories and hold no grudges against us. Typically, nothing gets hurt other than our ego. In contrast, if we make mistakes with our human relationships, then the effects can be quite damaging. If we neglect someone, or treat someone like an "object" to be practiced with, we may cause major, lasting damage to that person, as well as damage our own long-term reputation because we will become known as a "user." The stakes are higher, and the emotions stronger, when it comes to human relationships.

Normally, to keep from becoming overwhelmed by the high stakes of relationships, we offer different people different levels of relationship intensity, such as Figure 3-1 displays:

LOW ← → HIGH
Ignore   Politeness   Intimate
     Disinterested   Sincerity

Figure 3-1: Sample Degrees of Relationship Intensity

At the low end of the intensity range, we may choose to ignore interacting with strangers, such as when we ride in an elevator. Somewhere near the middle of the intensity range we might be willing to offer people, such as our work colleagues, polite levels of civil exchange by discussing harmless topics such as sports, movie stars, or hobbies. At the high end of relationship intensity, we are willing to exchange more personal information, such as our goals and our mistakes. Sometimes these confidants are family members. Sometimes they are friends. We distinguish our relationships by the depth and comfort level of information that we disclose to each other, with our closest allies typically being those with whom we comfortably share our deepest information. We become fiercely loyal to this "chosen family" of information sharers—sometimes more loyal than we are to our own, original family.

One type of "chosen relationship" has become legendary for its loyalty. Tragedies have been written about the loss of this relationship to death or betrayal. "Happily ever after" stories and movies have celebrated the successful fulfillment of this relationship. This relationship is, of course, the commitment of two people who pledge to live together, "until death do they part," in marriage. We will focus this chapter primarily on the various factors that impact how two such people might "come together." At the same time, these factors can also affect the "and stay together" bonds of married couples and good friends. The three significant questions that we wish to intelligently explore are:

Where does attraction come from?
What does "having sex" add to a relationship?
What does "making love" add to a relationship?

Before we begin, a brief philosophy about how we will explore the *Life* of relationships seems appropriate.

Thinking as a Scientist, not as a Lawyer

When we analyze a relationship, or anything else for that matter, we may use at least two different approaches. In the first approach, we may act as a Lawyer. Lawyers take a position and defend it. By virtue of their occupation, it is their job to present the best case that justifies why their position is correct. Lawyers strongly emphasize points that support their position, and neglect to mention contrary information. Lawyers, in an attempt to convince others, will use passion to persuade. The Lawyer might even be more interested in winning a case than in learning the actual truth or correct answer. For example, some Lawyers will defend a guilty person simply out of the belief that everyone deserves a good legal defense. It is quite possible that some guilty people have not been convicted because their defense Lawyer was better than the prosecuting Lawyer.

While the Lawyer approach is noble in certain situations, this method of analysis does little to aid our growth of relationship intelligence. In fact, defending only one side of a viewpoint can be dangerous. For example, consider what would happen if we viewed our relationships with only the one-sided question of "Why should I remain in this relationship?" Such an approach might blind us from considering if we should leave that relationship. As a result, we may stay in an energy-draining relationship even though we really should separate from it. Rather than justifying our relationship actions from just one viewpoint, we should review our relationships as a Scientist.

49

Scientists take a balanced approach to knowledge. A true Scientist starts with an opinion and then tests it to see if it is, in fact, true. Although Scientists would like their hypotheses to be proven true during their experiments and observations, Scientists remain committed to learning the truth, even if it means accepting that their original predictions were wrong. Rather than defend an incorrect opinion, Scientists drop their ego, accept new wisdom, and use the more accurate knowledge. Similarly, we must be open to the possibility that we will uncover a previously bad relationship choice. Such a mistake, if we learn from it, can improve our ability to predict the future. Unlike the Lawyer's debating approach, the Scientist's investigative approach gives us a better chance of uncovering the true causes of our outcomes—in this case, the causes of our relationship successes and failures.

To better uncover the causes of our relationship outcomes, we should acquire a basic understanding about a key factor in our romantic relationships—our brains. Yes, our brains. Paul MacLean popularized a three part model of the brain that helps provides such an understanding. This three-part brain, often called the "triune brain," looks something like Figure 3-2:

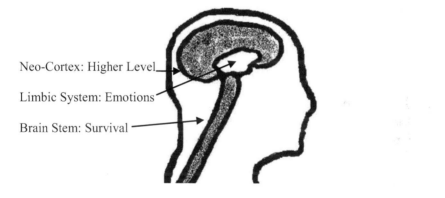

Figure 3-2: The Triune Brain

Figure 3-2 shows a simplified version of the three regions of our brain. Without diving too deeply into the realms of cognitive psychology and neuropsychology, it is a reasonable generalization to say that the oldest portion of the brain, the brain stem, processes our survival instincts, such as sleeping and procreating. The next layer of the brain—the limbic system—has been shown to provide us with an ability to feel and display emotions. Finally, in the highest, most recently developed portion of our brains, our neo-cortex layer allows us to understand abstract concepts such as symbols, written language, and non-concrete expressions such as "love" (more on that in a moment).

Some of the most actionable, choice-impacting insights into our relationship rituals will be gained by contrasting our brain stem <u>urges</u> with the <u>potential</u> <u>abilities</u> of our neo-cortex. For an exploration into the somewhat mysterious and beautiful influences of the limbic system, consider reading *A General Theory of Love* by Thomas Lewis, Fari Amini, and Richard Lannon.

Why Scientists must be Humble when explaining Attraction

Given our basic understanding of the regions of our brain, we can begin to intelligently explore a significant source of attraction. At the same time, to properly interpret the scientific studies about attraction, we must remember the principle of *range of quality*. This principle notes that "no one is average." Being "non-average" is an interesting phenomenon that frequently occurs whenever we investigate a characteristic of nature. For simplicity, consider the human characteristic of height. Suppose that scientific studies state that the average height of an adult U.S. male is five foot, ten inches (5'10"). If you were to take a sheet of paper and write down the heights of next 1,000 men that you saw, not all of the men would be 5'10". Many of them would be slightly taller or shorter than 5'10". A small minority would be really far from the average height—less than 5'2" or taller than 6'6". Overall, research suggests that the height of men would have a distribution similar to Chart 3-3:

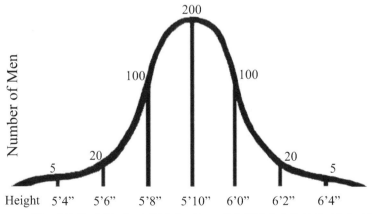

Chart 3-3: A Typical Distribution of 1,000 Adult U.S. Male Height

Chart 3-3 shows that the <u>largest</u> number of men (approximately 200) would be the average height of 5'10." At the same time, there would be many more men <u>who</u> <u>were</u> <u>not</u> 5'10" (approximately 800). Does this non-5'10" data negate the usefulness of our earlier information that the average male is 5'10"?

Certainly not. Chart 3-3 shows that many men, while not exactly 5'10", are within an inch or two of that height. The overall shape of Chart 3-3 is commonly known as "the bell curve." The bell-shaped "bump" reflects that many people approximately possess the average amount of a characteristic—in this case, "height." Most scientific analyses are conducted and reported based upon the characteristics of a population forming a bell curve shape.

However, few people are actually "average" in more than one trait. Consider how few males would actually be the average height of 5'10" while at the same time be the average weight of 182 lbs, with an average education of 13.1 years of schooling, working an average of 32.3 hours per week, and earning an average of $28,173.82 a year. No one is ever "completely average" in all characteristics. The individuality within any group of people creates a *range of quality* for any measured characteristic. For example, the characteristic of height might have a quality ranging from "short" to "tall." For the characteristic of wealth, the quality range might go from "poor" to "rich." So, as you read through the following pages on attraction, if you feel as though you, or the person that you are interested in, seems to have more sex drive, or less desire for money, or differ in quality from the other characteristics that are discussed, that is quite possible. The next section is simply designed to increase your intelligence about what the "average" 18-25 year old will find attractive. Individual circumstances and preferences will always vary, but they will also usually be close to the average.

What might average, Primitive "Attraction" look like?

Men and women differ in what they find, on average, to be most attractive about the opposite gender. As an <u>average</u> generalization of how their different attraction mechanisms work, you might wish to consider and compare how:

1) Men find women most attractive when the women are F.L.Y.
2) Women find men most attractive when the men are from A.S.I.A.

As you have probably already deduced, F.L.Y. and A.S.I.A. are acronym words—words whose letters each represent an individually separate word. Acronym words provide an easy way to remember information. We will start to understand the essence of attraction between men and women by first deconstructing what makes F.L.Y. women so attractive to men. We will then look at A.S.I.A. Having seen both sides of a common coin, we will be able to see how all of the attraction forces appear to revolve around the common principle of *procreation*—the *growth* of the human population. There is a strong set of evidence that what currently attracts us to members of the opposite gender—initially, at least—are the same features that once allowed our ancestors to be the most successful at producing children.

Stated more simply, we are descendents of people who were good at procreating. Those successful procreation strategies and urges have now become, even if unconsciously, strong impulses for each generation of people. Such procreative drives occur primarily in the most primitive part of our brain—our brain stem. Although the attraction mechanisms appear somewhat simplistic, they provide a compelling explanation about how an average person is attracted to a person of the opposite gender.

We will begin with the three F.L.Y. traits that represent what a primitive-focused man will prefer, whether he is aware of it or not, when he begins assessing a woman's partnership potential. Basically, the three attraction factors are based upon a woman's potential fertility.

"F" is for "faithful." For single women who have not yet entered a phase of "exclusive engagement" with a man, having a reputation of being a faithful female is advantageous. When a woman insults another woman by calling her "easy," a "slut," or a "whore," she is trying to create a damaging reputation that will make men less likely to believe that the "slut" is capable of being faithful in the long-term. The "whore" might appear to be physically fertile (as the "L" and "Y" letters will show in a second), but if a man believes that she would not be faithful, then that man might also perceive that the children she would "produce" might not include his genetic contribution. Unfaithful is unattractive.

Now, a woman can still "sleep around" and attract men, but what kind of men? The quality range of men goes from "one night stand" partners to "long-term commitment" partners. Women who "sleep around" may unknowingly signal that they want "one night stand" partners. There are many primitively focused males who will answer such signals.

Thus, a "sleep around" reputation will negatively affect a woman who is trying to attract a long-term commitment male. The men who interact with a "sleep around" woman might be inclined to wonder "if she is this easy to seduce, how many other sex partners has she had?" and "if she is this loose, then maybe she does not value physical relationships any more than non-physical…wait a minute, does she even value me?"

The average man's simultaneous urge for a "sleep around" woman and a long-term fidelity partner, as well as the conflict that it causes, has been labeled as "The Madonna Whore complex." It describes how long-term men want a Madonna—a woman as wholesome as the Virgin Mother of Christ. At the same time, the average man's urges also makes him want a "whore" for short-term, right now, gratification. Women choose the type of men that they will attract by the part of a man's wants that they aim to satisfy.

Indeed, if a woman wants to become a "target" of a group of average young men, then she should publicly state that she is a "virgin." The virgin status reflects fidelity. Virginity represents an unblemished host for a male's genetics and is a highly-prized asset. Society reflects this desire for a pure female when weddings showcase brides dressed in the pure, virgin color of white. At the same time, other parts of society—typically the parts that want your money—work hard to convince you that casual sex is no big deal and is, contrary to social reputations, worth pursuing.

The next letter of F.L.Y.—"L"—is for "looks." There are many discussions about what it means to look attractive. Male poets have often pondered what part of a woman's body is the most attractive: Her eyes? Her bosom? Her gluteus maximus? Interestingly, research by Devendra Singh suggests that there appears to be one female feature that is highly agreed upon as attractive (by both men and women). This feature has the dimension of "00.7," and makes a woman look somewhat like a James Bond girl. This feature can be found in hard-bodied, athletic women as well as softer-bodied, full-figured gals. This "00.7" dimension is the ratio of a female's waist to her hips. For example, for a woman with the dimensions 32-24-35, her waist-to-hip ratio of 24/35 equals 00.69, almost the precise ratio of "attractiveness."

What is it about a female's lower body ratio that enhances her attractiveness? One possible answer is associated with a female's appearance of pregnancy potential. If the primitive portion of a male's brain and genetics are geared toward finding partners who can produce offspring for him, then the "00.7" women are more likely to look as though they are unfertilized and able to become pregnant. In contrast, obese women look more like they are already pregnant with someone else's child.

It seems odd that something as simple as weight could affect attraction so negatively, yet our society certainly reflects the "L" factor. For example, when discussions in male locker rooms at health clubs include favorable reviews of women who have an attractive "hour glass figure" and "curves that are kickin'," they are indirectly referencing the "00.7" ratio. Is this attraction factor superficial and simplistic? Possibly, although waist-to-hip ratios of 0.8 or less are usually associated with healthier women, so the "look" could be a primitive attraction for a <u>healthy</u>, fertile female. Does "the look" have anything to do with the deeper value of a woman's character? Maybe, as it might reflect that a woman has the self-awareness and discipline to take care of her body. Controversial or not, the average primitive male seeks a "00.7" woman.

"Y" is for youth. With the procreation potential for women beginning with the menstrual cycles of their teenage years and lasting into their 40s, if men desire to grow their genetic lineage, then they primitively stack the odds of procreative success in their favor by seeking out younger women. Statistics show that the older a woman becomes, the lower her success at bearing children. Younger women are more fertile.

U.S. consumer products reflect this demand for younger, or at least younger-looking, women. Cosmetics industries offer anti-aging creams that reduce wrinkles. Manufacturers of exercise equipment promise toned muscles of teenage tightness. Health spas provide anti-flabby skin treatments. At the extreme, liposuction and other cosmetic surgeries allow women to retain a more youthful look, and maintain a "00.7" waist-hip ratio. Even with all of these anti-aging methods, it seems rare to find a major Hollywood film star who is female, older than age 40, and a solo headlining star. In contrast, there are many major movie stars who are male and over the age of 40. An interesting intersection of Hollywood and the cosmetic surgery business can be found by watching the television series *Dr. 90210*.

Becoming F.L.Y.

To some extent, women have the ability to manipulate their own F.L.Y. factors, on average, if they wish to make attracting a man a priority. For example, developing a reputation as a faithful partner is a matter of choice and will power. Additionally, youthful, "00.7" looks can be achieved through lifestyle choices. Exercises such as leg squats and lunges develop a woman's legs and derriere into firm, youthful looking muscle, creating an hour glass figure along her lower body. Bench press, back rows, and shoulder raise exercises add to a woman's upper hour glass shape, and aerobic exercise shrinks one's waistline. Calorie awareness can also lower the waist number, while clothing can be chosen to accentuate a woman's "00.7" ratio of waist-to-hip curves. Wrinkled skin can be minimized by drinking lots of water, not smoking, and minimizing exposure to the sun. As with all exercise and health plans, consider consulting with a physician or other trained expert (i.e., nutritionist) to discuss your individual plans and goals.

The one youth factor that science has not yet been able to manipulate at a cheap rate for women, or their husbands, is the cost of time. Societal phrases such as "her biological time clock is ticking" reflect how single women can begin to feel an unfair pressure from the decreasing fertility of their 30s. Currently, fertility clinics increase the odds of successful fertilization for women, but positive results are not guaranteed. Fertility treatments can (at the time of this writing) easily cost $10,000. Time is a rather daunting factor that a woman must consider as she decides whether or not it is time to get serious about looking for a long-term partner.

A.S.I.A.

With regard to what primitive women are looking for in men, they are seeking men from A.S.I.A. More specifically, A.S.I.A. is a way for women to stack the odds in their favor that they will commit, theoretically through marriage, to a man who will have enough resources to be able to properly care for her. This is not to imply that women need men in order to live. Rather, the A.S.I.A. attraction urge seems to be a genetic leftover from the historical development of the human race. Imagine that there was once a time of "hunting and gathering" tribes of people, when only men were the leaders. The tribal split of food, clothing, and shelter amongst the clan of people was based upon the physical ability and contribution of each member. Men were more likely to perform the more physically dangerous tasks, and therefore men received more of the resources. If a woman became pregnant, then she would become physically limited by her pregnancy during months eight and nine, as well as the first six weeks after childbirth. During this time she would not be able to contribute very much to the community. As a result, she would have depended on her male partner to be able to provide the resources that would support her and, eventually, her newborn child during the key birth months. With this as a primitive woman's motivation, the A.S.I.A. factors now become more apparent:

"A" is for age. An older man, on average, earns more each year compared to a younger man. This higher earnings, and therefore higher access to resources, is attractive to a "modern day," primitive woman who has a *Life* plan that involves her becoming a mom at some time in the future, especially if she has hopes to leave the workforce for a period of months or years to raise children. First-time American marriages reflect this "the man is older bias" by approximately two years, with men being nearly 27 years of age when they first marry, and women being approximately 25.

"S" is for status. The more accomplished a man is, the more likely it is that he has high earnings and access to more resources. These accomplishments can even be based upon future "potential." Think about your high school days. Which scenario was more likely:

1) A male, sophomore student dating a female, senior student.
2) A male, senior student dating a female, sophomore student.

Most likely, you would have seen senior males dating sophomore or junior girls. Senior girls were more likely to be dating senior boys, or even college freshmen boys. This coincides with the pattern that an older male has accomplished more and has a "higher than average" status among high school males. The high school senior male is also closer to becoming an independent adult and either going to college or earning a significant paycheck from the "real world"—both major signs of status that would lead an average, younger female to feel attraction.

"I" is for intelligence. Have you ever noticed how you will sometimes find a smart, wealthy man with a ridiculously beautiful, but mentally deficient, woman? In contrast, I have not yet encountered…ever… a smart woman who was in a long-term relationship with a dumb man. This difference in each gender's demand for an intelligent mate can be explained. Whereas the ancestral caveman was risking relatively little if he were to make a woman pregnant, that woman was risking her body and her life. The woman had a much higher motivation to seek out a man who appeared intelligent enough to be a good protector and provider.

Times have changed, even if our average historical urges have not. For a woman, pregnancy still includes a high opportunity cost. A woman's ability to accomplish tasks, such as advancing in school or in her career, can be greatly reduced if she becomes pregnant outside of a secure, marriage partnership. Therefore, a woman generally needs to feel as though a man could support her with at least the same level of luxury that she would have attained on her own. In order to do this, the male partner most likely needs to be at least as smart as the woman, if not smarter. Also, statistically speaking, the more formal education a male has, the more likely he is to have higher earnings, and therefore a greater access to resources. Intelligence enhances a man's attractiveness.

"A" is for ambition. In the past, I have asked my female students the following scenario: Imagine that you are at a New Year's Eve dance party. As you walk past a group of 25+ year-olds, you hear a reasonably attractive guy say the following, "Wow, am I in a big time, financial bind! My used car just broke down, and my college loans are coming due next month..." This opening communication is not a very good first impression for most casual listeners. However, suppose that you had to linger around for another second or two, maybe because you had to adjust your shoe. During that time, you happen to hear that same young man say "Thank goodness I will finish that MBA at Harvard this spring..." Given that the average person who has earned an MBA at Harvard will earn a starting salary of around $150,000 (in the year 2008 dollar values), do you think that this piece of information might make the young man more attractive to the average female? My students have consistently answered, "Yes." Does that mean that the primitive female is a superficial "gold digger?" No. This is only an initial urge of attraction, not the final commitment criteria.

A.S.I.A. Magnetism

Interestingly, men have the ability to enhance their own A.S.I.A. factors, on average, if they wish to make attracting a woman a priority. Also, much like women, these changes take a little bit of time to achieve. Developing A.S.I.A. factors allows a man to use a principle known as *pull versus push*.

This principle of *pull versus push* contrasts two different approaches. With the push strategy, you try to "push" yourself or your ideas onto someone. For example, a male might try to display his resources or status by buying dinner for his date, or he might try to display his intelligence through witty comments, jokes or charismatic insights. In U.S. society, although females can offer hints of interest, the majority of the pressure to start a relationship still falls on the man. If a man and a woman are total strangers, and no friends have given either of them hints about the other's reputation, then their initial meeting probably involves the man "pushing" and promoting himself. Looking a bit like a Lawyer, he will try to suggest reasons why she should date him.

In contrast, those men with a magnetic "pull" have already achieved some type of status before they meet new women. By having already achieved something notable, the male is more likely to meet females who already recognize his status, which raises his attractiveness within their primitive rating system. Consider the phenomenon of teenage boy bands. Imagine if any of these MTV or Hollywood stars paused during one of their concerts to ask a shrieking teenage fan for a date. The singer would barely be able to say "Would you like to go out…" before the female would jump over the railing and into his arms. Yet pick any teen idol, or look at *People's* "Sexiest Man of the Year" candidates, and ask yourself, "If that guy were my brother (or cousin, or uncle), and not some accomplished entertainer, would he really be that attractive?" Although most celebrities would at least be classified as "not ugly," many are also not amazingly gorgeous. Their body types differ as well. What these men do have in common are their achievements. By now you have probably noticed that there is no "L" in A.S.I.A.. Females, on average, are in agreement about the attractiveness of men due to their resources, but females do not show as strong of an agreement on the issue of "looks."

For men (or women) wanting to charge up their magnetic "pull," they might consider doing something interesting that would allow them to easily share stories with strangers who approach them. For example, they could:

- Practice interesting hobbies: sky diving, painting, rock climbing….
- Take grand adventures: travel, study an international culture…
- Pursue difficult goals: millionaire by age 50, train for a marathon …
- Be charitable: volunteer to build houses for Habitat for Humanity…

It seems deceptively simple, yet the pattern stands firm: if you want to be an interesting person, then go do something interesting. If you want to be seen as important, then do something important. For insights into a lesser known individual who has been building up his magnetism, consider reading *Three Cups of Tea*. It is the story of how one man, Greg Mortensen, has been battling terrorism and changing the nations of Pakistan and Afghanistan by bringing schools to the native people.

With a strong magnetism earned, you do not have to worry about seeming like a pushy Lawyer during a date. I observed such humbleness a few years ago when I joined a new work group. As I was meeting with everyone during the first day, I asked people about their background. One colleague, Rob, said "I went to b-school in Massachusetts." I thought nothing of it at the time—he said he went to a business school. A few days later someone else told me how impressed he had been with Rob, "who went to business school in Massachusetts...at that little place called Harvard." Rob's professional status, which he earned, was a powerful example of magnetic pull. Many people bragged about Rob. Rob's work performance and results had earned him a reputation as a high quality guy. Additionally, once people found out that Rob was single, it was not surprising that people tried to set him up with up every high quality, single female that they knew. Rob was "a catch." He was "magnetic pull" personified.

Another factor that a man can leverage is his age. With each year, an average man has the opportunity to develop his intelligence. He might complete more education and acquire a higher paying job. Alternatively, he might work at a second job for a year or two, and save up all of the extra money so that he could purchase more resources. Those accomplishments would bring status. With status, his confidence and ambition would grow. It is the confident male who finds it easiest to meet females—he is comfortable and confident about himself. When women say that they find confident men sexy, there is a plausible link that the man's confidence represents his resource potential. One might even hypothesize that the reason women often wait for a man to ask them out, as opposed to the woman asking the man out, is that the "female waiting process" screens out the low confidence, lesser accomplished men. Occasionally, men will act as "players" and boast a bit more about themselves than they merit, but such fakers are usually uncovered with time.

Imagine that we revisit our New Year's Eve party. This time a woman asks a man "What do you do in the daytime?" Rather than focusing on creative comebacks or lame "pick up" lines, consider how different this man's first impression to the woman would be if he could legitimately respond, "I continue to work on becoming a millionaire by age 50, and I keep my eyes open for the right kind of person who would like to join me on that journey." By building up their earnings intelligence, such as with the intelligence of the earlier *Money* chapter, and by using the money-focusing tool taught in the upcoming *Time* chapter, men—and women—each have the ability to credibly offer that "become a millionaire" response.

In a simplistic world, if we were only a function of our urges, then all men would seek fertile-looking trophy wives and all women would want resource-rich trophy husbands. Many people suspected that this type of lower-brain attraction formed the basis of billionaire J. Howard Marshall's marriage to former Playboy model Vickie Lynn Marshall (also known as "Anna Nicole Smith"). The billionaire Marshall, who was more than 60 years older than Smith, had acquired status through his oil business. For her part, Smith certainly offered youthful, fertile-looking qualities that a primitive male instinct would desire. In 2010, another F.L.Y.—A.S.I.A relationship appeared to form when model Crystal Harris became engaged to Playboy founder Hugh Hefner. Hugh was 60 years older than Crystal.

Of course, this primitive level of attraction does not apply across all of the ranges of relationships. There are almost always exceptions to nearly any predictive model, even the model of F.L.Y.—A.S.I.A. Once, when I was presenting this model to some of my students, a group of them pointed out that the Hollywood couple of Demi Moore and Ashton Kutcher did not match up with the F.L.Y.—A.S.I.A. model. Demi was already "resource accomplished," as well as 15 years older than Ashton when they met. This negated most of the average F.L.Y.—A.S.I.A factors. I thanked the students for pointing out an exception to "the rule." Sadly, the couple later divorced.

"On average," F.L.Y.—A.S.I.A. offers a reasonable generalization of the complimentary relationship between a woman's fertility, a man's resources, and their combined, procreative growth potential. Many more details, in a reader-friendly format, of the different gender motivations of attraction can be found in books such as *The Evolution of Desire* by David Buss and *The Mating Mind* by Geoffrey Miller. We will uncover ways to build relationships that are stronger than these primitive foundations as this *Life* book continues.

Potential Consequences of Primitive Urges

Consider the following dating scenario:

A wealthy looking, athletic man invites a friendly, fit woman out for a dinner date. He chooses a fancier restaurant, and picks up the woman in his luxury vehicle. While at dinner, he asks her questions about her goals, and he explains some of his grander dreams, including how he will one day become a millionaire. After dinner, she invites him back to her place. They drink wine together, enjoying each other's company, and laugh late into the night. They become slightly tipsy from the alcohol, and thoroughly intoxicated by each other's personality. The man tries an aggressive flirting move with the woman, telling her in poetic verse how he would like to "make love" to her. Aroused by the passions of the evening's events, the woman takes the man's hand and the two of them proceed to her bedroom.

Given what we know about the F.L.Y.—A.S.I.A. factors of attraction, this "dinner and a one night stand" scenario suddenly appears to be a superficial, "civilized" form of brain stem autopilot. It was not just chivalry that compelled the man to display his resources with both his money and with his attention to her interests—the man also showed that he was self-confident by being able to talk about topics other than himself. She, in return, dazzled him with her looks and, ultimately, shared a portion of her procreative abilities with him. For some part of our bell curve population, this "civilized prostitution contract" is acceptable. For others, this appears to be about as evolved as two lizards blindly acting out their urges. A reality-TV series that exploited these urges was *Joe Millionaire*. Watch it and enjoy the F.L.Y.—A.S.I.A. factors in action! Alternatively, if you can find a copy of the show *Who Wants to Marry a Multi-Millionaire?*, you will see similar patterns of behavior.

We now move toward a higher-level brain evaluation of romantic relationships by investigating two phrases that are used casually, and often incorrectly, as substitutes for one another—"having sex" and "making love." This journey of growth takes us from our primitive brain stem's attraction approach to a more intelligent, neo-cortex level.

What does "Having Sex" Add to a Relationship?

Before we tap into our higher neo-cortex abilities to explore the abstract topic of "love," we should acknowledge how the procreative act of sex affects a relationship. Adding sexual intercourse to a relationship, either before or after marriage, increases the relationship's intensity. On the positive side, creating orgasms for each member of a couple can be a strong bonding experience, at least in the beginning. However, just as sexual encounters raise the potential rewards of a relationship, they also increase the risks. For example, consider the difference in break ups between two couples—one that has included sexual intercourse, and one that has not. Those individuals who have shared coitus experiences often feel more painful emotions of loss or betrayal when their relationship ends. Meanwhile, those couples who have not slept together, and eventually learn that they are not compatible, are more likely to find that their relationship breakups are disappointing, but far less draining.

Since it is a primitive act, sex is one of the lowest common denominators on which to build a relationship. As powerful as it can be in creating a relationship bond, sexual attraction can fail as a long-term tool for keeping a couple together. Individuals who have broken up with former sex-mates have later been known to say things like "the sex was great, but I could not stand how he thought he was never wrong" and "the sex was great, but she drove me away because she always just wanted to talk about herself." Clearly, there are higher priorities that keep a couple together beyond the initial, primitive attractions. Yet the primitive drive to procreate is so powerful in the average person that it can distract a person from building a relationship based on more advanced attraction criteria.

To gain an idea of just how blinding sexual attraction can be, consider performing the following experiment: Ask 10 or more divorced people one simple question—"Did you engage in sex with your ex-spouse before marriage?" People's responses might sound something like "Well yes, but that had nothing to do with our divorce. He (or she) changed." These responses may sound like one-sided Lawyer arguments, with the people acting as though their primitive sex drives did not affect their relationship judgments—nobody wants to feel as though they were shallow and overwhelmed by their primitive urges.

Besides this interview experiment, you might choose to read scientific studies on the outcomes of un-wed relationship behaviors, such as those that were intensified by couples choosing to live together. Let us assume that choosing such a cohabitation relationship includes sexual encounters (a fairly reasonable assumption). If so, then the corresponding research appears to predict that the primitive act of sex destabilizes the development of a lasting relationship. For example, William Axinn and Arland Thornton noted that when cohabitation precedes marriage, those marriages were 50 to 100 percent more likely to dissolve than those marriages that were not preceded by cohabitation.

Although cohabitation sex does not appear to lead to stronger marriages, strong marriages do appear to lead to better sex. For example, a group of researchers at the University of Chicago found that married people have most sex (and the most orgasmic). The evidence that compares married, unmarried, and cohabiting people supports that those who are able to develop good marriages are more likely to lead happier lives. The short-term gratifications from "sleeping around," and the sexual encounters of cohabitation, seem to reduce the odds of producing a good marriage foundation.

However, the short-term gratifications of sexual encounters do offer couples another outcome. Oddly enough, this outcome rarely gets included in public presentations of sex. Perhaps a Lawyer convinced the novelists and movie makers that people would be more inclined to view and buy products if only F.L.Y.—A.S.I.A. desires were used. The unstated outcome from F.L.Y.—A.S.I.A. gratifications is the chance that a sexual encounter will create a new life. Although a sexual encounter is not long lasting, the emotions attached to it, especially if it later includes dealing with an unexpected pregnancy, might be. Mary Beth Whitehead, the original abortion client in the *Roe v. Wade* Supreme Court case, had an abortion and regretted it. Indeed, more than a few people have felt immense guilt and suffering as a result of their abortion actions. Intelligent people must remember that there is a procreative outcome that completes the natural function of a sexual encounter. The encounter that leads to that outcome is not to be confused with "love." We explore the distinct status of "love" next.

What does "Making Love" Add?

To begin achieving relationships that are more meaningful than those of a lizard's autopilot, we need to start using our higher level portion of the brain. As a blunt, but useful, first attempt at evaluating our relationships for higher qualities, we must develop a concept for the abstract, overly-used, expression known as "love."

Understanding the principle of *love* can be complicated because the term "love" has been casually used in so many ways. For example, someone may say that they "love" chocolate ice cream, or that they "love" certain things about their partner. Yet these uses of the word "love" merely reflect a taste preference. You could substitute the phrase "really like" for this use of "love." This is not the principle of *love*.

Another way that "love" gets framed is as an emotion, as in "falling in love" or "falling out of love." This definition of "love" permits "love" to be a temporary mood, and sounds as though it is something beyond our control. This definition is more like a "feeling of attraction." Such a feeling could fade with time because the primitive portion of our mind can become easily distracted by other F.L.Y. bodies or A.S.I.A. resource providers. For example, consider the 40+ year old man who goes through a "mid-life crisis." At the extreme, he divorces his 40+ year old wife (she is no longer as fertile looking) and spends lavish amounts of money (portions of his accumulated resources) on a 20-something year old girlfriend (who is quite fertile looking). His actions of "falling in love again" do not follow the principle of *love*.

One other use of the term "love" is as a substitute for "with good intentions." For example, consider the type of mother who constantly tries to provide for her child. Unfortunately, she ends up being <u>too</u> <u>much</u> of a provider and, as a result, constantly spoils her child. This selfish child eventually develops a volcanic personality that erupts with disappointment and conflict whenever it does not get what it wants. When the mother is questioned about why she spoiled her child, one response might be "I did it out of love." This is an example of ignorant action, but it is not the principle of *love*.

What, then, is *love*? If achieving a *loving* relationship is the summit of a couple's travels together, then the acronym S.U.M.A. summarizes the key aspects of *love*. Pronounced "sooh-mah," it is an easy way to consider viewing the intensity and summit of a relationship. *Love* is a *Selfless, Universal, Moral, Action.* These four elements require some elaboration.

The "selfless" portion of *love* can be a bit deceptive at first because *love* has been overly romanticized with regards to certain sacrifices. Many of us would be willing to "take a bullet" for a loved one. We might even push a total stranger out of the way of an oncoming car. Such love is noble, valiant, and gains us tremendous public recognition. These romantic "deaths" have an attractive quality about them.

However, fewer people are as excited about performing a lesser praised, selfless "death." For example, some married people find it unacceptable to "die" in their career by turning down a promotion, even if the additional hours and travel associated with that promotion would take more time away from their family life. Similarly, other people avoid lower paying jobs, even if the jobs locations would benefit their spouse. Providing spouses with opportunities such as better work, further schooling, or a closer proximity to other family members does not appear to some people as acts of love—career "deaths" are not as attractive as career-building steps that result in pay raises, company recognition, and a bigger ego. "Selfless death" is hard to do. The boyfriend who encourages his girlfriend to go to the best college or job that she can, even though it might be far away from him and reduce his chances of seeing her, is performing love. So, too, are the parents that raise their children, yet expect no payback for all of their years of sacrifice. Like most worthwhile endeavors, being selfless is not easy to do.

When it comes to the "universal" nature of *love, love* is the same universal principle that appears in many different forms. For example, colorfully speaking, imagine that *love* is a warming yellow, sun-like color. Imagine also that the action of "respecting authority" appears as the conservative color blue. If we *love* our parents, and our "yellow" of *love* is combined with the respectful energy of "blue," then our relationship with our parents would appear to other people as a "green" relationship (just as the rainbow mix of yellow + blue = green).

Alternatively, if we *love* our spouse (or fiancé, or serious boyfriend or girlfriend) and also have a fiery passion of "red" for them, then our relationship would appear to outsiders as a glowing orange color (yellow + red = orange).

The orange and green appearances of our relationships make them look quite distinct to outside observers. The contrast is due to the unique people and interactive elements that occur within each relationship. Yet if outside observers separated out the non-love elements, such as respect and passion, then the remaining essence of warming, yellow *love* would look the same across all relationships.

The next component of *love*—the "moral" aspect—might be the hardest aspect of S.U.M.A. love to achieve. It requires using your neo-cortex to sort out your standards of praiseworthy (a.k.a. "moral") acts. While individual standards for moral behavior may vary, there are certainly some minimal standards of good and bad behavior. For example, we should feel comfortable stopping a friend or a romantic partner from drinking and driving. We do not want drunken people to compromise their safety, as well as the safety of their passengers or other travelers. Our action to take away someone's keys may result in us being unpopular for a while, yet for reasons of love we would perform this action. *Love* requires that we hold our loved ones to standards of moral behavior. The ancient Greeks might have described this love as *philia*—a type of "virtuous care"—not to be confused with the passionate feelings of *eros*.

Thus, the morality associated with "making love" is distinct from the act of "having sex." Morality allows us to ask questions about the way that we interact with our romantic partners. Morality does not ask if men and women could engage in sexual acts. Instead, it asks us to decide under what circumstances men and women should engage in sexual acts. For example, is it really an expression of love if two people engage in sex when one of them is just starting college, or some other *Life-Altering* journey? Primitive urges aside, under what conditions should two people be sexual with one another? "When married" is a no-brainer, if both voluntarily engage in the act.

Outside of marriage, sex in a relationship becomes trickier to defend, from a S.U.M.A. love perspective. Is a man really looking out for the woman's best interest by exposing her to the chance of becoming pregnant with a new *Life*? Perhaps if he is strongly committed to her, this may seem like an acceptable risk. Of course, if the man were so strong about his commitment to the woman, why has he not proposed to her yet?

Some young men will respond to questions about their sexual morality by saying "I do have her best interest at heart...I use a condom." Gentlemen, and ladies, two secular responses to consider:

1) Gentlemen, condoms do not always work. I have met dads who swear to this. The woman is still exposed to the "risk" of pregnancy.

2) Ladies, there is a strong argument that birth control measures were a primitive man's selfish, albeit intelligent, way of turning women into civilized prostitutes. More specifically, men are now able to engage in sex by committing only a tiny part of their resources, enough to enchant a woman to a bedroom. This lowers the moral behavior that both genders expect of each other. Perhaps this is why unmarried people have less satisfying sex—there is less engagement and fulfillment, and more lower, primitive levels of attempted gratification. There is no trust, or authentic intimacy.

"Action" is the final element of *love*. People occasionally have difficulty recognizing appropriate, *loving* actions, because the emotionally appealing phrase "give and take" conjures up expectations that all portions of all relationships are two-way streets of bargaining. True *love* is only a one-way street of action. Donating food to a homeless shelter is an obvious example of this one-way action of love. A writer named Paul once wrote about the one-way action of love in a letter to the Corinthians:

Love is patient, Love is kind.
It is not jealous. It is not pompous. It is not inflated. It is not rude.
It does not seek its own interests.
It is not quick-tempered. It does not brood over injury.

It does not rejoice over wrongdoing but rejoices with the Truth.
Love bears all things, believes all things, hopes all things,
endures all things.
Love never fails.

Some people expect something in return for their "love." This expectation is a form of "trading," not loving. Certainly, we hope that we date, and presumably marry, someone who will love us as well, and treat us with the decency deserved by all people. Still, it is our commitment to love someone that should guide us when controversial situations arise.

For example, it can be very difficult to have a conversation with someone when they have insulted us. People may accidentally say things in ways that make us feel inferior or hurt. If we do not choose to act in a loving manner toward these people, then we may respond to them by speaking an insult, or choosing to withdraw from the conversation. Alternatively, if we are committed to treating people in a loving way, then we will not respond with harmfully intended words, but instead will rise above the pain, and treat these people with decency. This action can calm heated situations, and maintain an open communication channel. Just remember, sometimes the burdening action of an "ego death" or "not having the last word" might fall upon your intelligent self, while the other person lashes out. No one ever said that love was easy!

Of course, sometimes love demands that we leave a relationship. If our partner repeatedly takes advantage of our love, and shows no signs of S.U.M.A. love toward us, then we need to strongly consider leaving such a relationship. For example, consider the boyfriends who cheat on their girlfriends. By any standard of morality, the girlfriends have the right to leave these types of relationships. However, sometimes a woman "fights for her man" because she believes that she can restore him back to moral behavior. Such efforts are noble, yet if the man continues his immoral behavior, and shows no signs of improvement, she must consider leaving the relationship. Sometimes, leaving is the only way that a man can understand that his choices are not acceptable to a woman. Detaching from such a non-S.U.M.A. relationship is not the same as "quitting," especially if it was done out of love and self-respect.

*****

Thus far, we have devoted our first three chapters to uncovering the more visible controls of our *Life* ship. In this chapter we explored the broad components of primitive *attraction*, looked at some of the consequences of *sex*, and developed a standard of *love* that could be used to gain further insight into the relationships to which we should attach or detach. We saw that "having sex" fades in its ability to keep couples together, while "making love" in a S.U.M.A. sense—which did not require sexual acts—can strengthen relationships over time.

With this foundation of relationship intelligence, we will use our next two chapters to expand our higher level, neo-cortex abilities within the less obvious *Life* choices of *Time* and *Values*. Each chapter will reveal additional, higher level ways of approaching relationships and money.

Additional Principles:

Range of Quality
Pull vs. Push
S.U.M.A. Love

For Further Reflection:

1) What do you and your friends find most attractive about men and women?

2) Are there people you know who have acted like F.L.Y.—A.S.I.A. primitives? By the way they dressed? By what they drove? By the way they dated?

3) What is the most selfless act of *love* that you have witnessed in a romantic relationship? In a non-romantic relationship?

4) What are your standards for moral / "praiseworthy" behavior? What are your minimum expectations of interaction within your romantic relationships?

Examples:
A one week vacation as a couple every year (maybe less with kids)?
Never drunk / always neo-cortex-like whenever around one another?

Couple's activities at least every other weekend?

5) Have you ever seen someone acting moral even when it meant that they would be unpopular? Have you ever had to act morally at the risk of popularity?

6) What do you think people should be willing to compromise, or prioritize, for the sake of their relationship?

For Further Investigation:

George Valliant, *Aging Well*

Dean Ornish, *Love and Survival*

Marriage statistics referenced from: Bramlett MD and Mosher WD. *Cohabitation, Marriage, Divorce, and Remarriage in the United States.* National Center for Health Statistics. Vital Health Stat 23(22). 2002.

Thomas Lewis, Fari Amini, and Richard Lannon, *A General Theory of Love*

Devendra Singh, "Adaptive significance of Female Physical Attractiveness: Role of Waist-to-Hip Ratio." *Journal of Personality and Social Psychology*, 1993.

Devendra Singh, "Ideal Female Body Shape: Role of Body Weight and Waist-to-Hip Ratio," *International Journal of Eating Disorders*, 1994.

Dr. 90210 has been found (usually) on the E! television network.

Married Age Statistics from: U.S. Census Bureau, American Community Survey 2002-2003, Census Supplementary Survey 2000-2001.

Mortensen and David Kelin, *Three Cups of Tea*

David Buss, *The Evolution of Desire*

Geoffrey Miller, *The Mating Mind*

Fox Television, *Joe Millionaire*

Fox Television, *Who Wants to Marry a Multi-Millionaire?*

William Axinn and Arland Thornton, "The Relationship Between Cohabitation and Divorce: Selectivity or Casual Influence?" *Demography*, Vol. 29, 1992.

"Sex in America" University of Chicago Study, *Time*, Oct. 17, 1994.

Robert Michael, John Gagnon, and Edward Lauman *Sex in America: A Definitive Survey*, 1994.

Time: The Ally of "Essence"

"You cannot step into the same river twice." — Heraclitus

The following is a timely tale to test your talent:

Imagine that it is the year 480 BC. You, an Athenian, have just been named the captain of a brand new ship called *The Autoscop*. The ship, constructed of 100 wooden planks, performs well as an Athenian patrol boat during its first year. At the end of that year, you notice that ten of the wooden boards of *The Autoscop* need to be replaced. As a result, you go to a seaport and replace the boards, and then head back out to the water to perform your patrolling mission...

Question: Would you rename *The Autoscop*? The question can be restated with greater details of motivation, perhaps as, "Has the replacement of those ten boards changed the boat so much that you would feel awkward if you continued calling the ship by its original name?" You might feel that this is a silly question—ten boards do not constitute a fundamental "change" to the ship. Therefore, let us assume that you make no name changes, and you start your second year of patrol duty.

During that second year you discover that ten more of the original planks need to be replaced. Once again, you take the ship into a port, make the replacements, and head back out to the sea. Do you still think that *The Autoscop* should keep the same name? You might still be inclined to say "Yes."

Yet consider what would happen if this pattern of replacing ten original boards occurred each year, for the next eight years, of the patrolling mission.

Although the replacement process would be gradual, at the end of those years all 100 of the ship's original planks would have been replaced. Would you still call the ship *The Autoscop*?

Let us test the ship's identity one other way. Imagine that, during each of those ten years, when you docked your ship for repairs, the ten new boards were sold to you by the same craftsman. Unknown to you, after you left each time, that craftsman then repaired the ten boards that you had discarded. Suppose that, at the end of ten years, the craftsman reassembled all 100 planks of wood into their original ship form. The craftsman then sailed that ship out to the harbor, next to where your current boat called *The Autoscop* was docked. Which of the two ships would deserve to be called *The Autoscop*? How would you decide?

The questions about *The Autoscop* highlight how difficult it can be for us to determine if an object or being has maintained a common identity across changing times. Think back to when you were a child, and see if you can recall when you first learned that a butterfly was once a caterpillar. The transformation process was an eye-opening experience for many of us. Although the changes in our lives are not likely to be as rapid or as dramatic as the caterpillar, our *Lives* will constantly experience change. As Heraclitus noted in the introductory quote to this chapter, you cannot step into the same river (of *Life*) twice, because a river is always flowing and changing.

At the same time, there does exist a common "essence" to most entities, including rivers. For example, consider the Nile River. Although the river has changed its form and shape somewhat since it was first named, most people still know what you are referring to if you use the label "Nile River." Similarly, although the exterior identity of a caterpillar changes, its essence of a life remains intact. Our vessel of a body and our pursuit of priorities will also change numerous times. These changes will challenge our ability to focus on achieving successful outcomes. Yet with an intelligent approach to *Life*, we can create and maintain an essence that produces successful outcomes.

Research has shown that positive outcomes are associated with certain behaviors. For example, consider an experiment that was conducted by Walter Mischel in the 1960s. Four year-old children took turns entering a room in which a researcher sat behind a desk. The researcher would then give the child a marshmallow and a choice. The first choice was that the four-year old could eat the marshmallow. As a second choice, the four year-old was told that the researcher had to briefly leave the room, and if the child did not eat the marshmallow and waited until the researcher returned, then that four year-old would be given an additional marshmallow.

Some children waited for the researcher to return (which may have taken 15 minutes or more). Other children did not wait. Researchers recorded who waited, and who did not, and then continued to observe the children as they grew older. The researchers discovered that those children who had waited for the researcher to return were more likely to achieve greater positive outcomes as teenagers, including scoring higher on their SATs and being identified as "more dependable." Additional outcomes associated with this "marshmallow experiment" can be found in books such as Daniel Goleman's *Emotional Intelligence*.

The preceding evidence suggests that we benefit by understanding how our actions, over time, lead to certain outcomes. Seeing the longer term outcome of an action may strengthen our ability to avoid the distraction of short-term gratifications. Thus, we will devote this chapter to exploring ways of leveraging time to our advantage. Although it is less obvious in its impact than money or relationships, time magnifies the gains and losses from our four control choices. With time, you can develop better relationship choices. For example, time offers you the chance to view a romantic relationship beyond the initial F.L.Y.—A.S.I.A. urges. This same, longer-term thinking can also be applied to increase your monetary wealth. The better you can identify a common essence that you want to develop across your *Life* (i.e., "growing to become a millionaire," "being a good relationship partner"), the more likely you will be able to focus your controls toward achieving that essence.

Alternatively, if you choose to ignore the use of longer-term perspectives, then you may one day experience a "mid-Life crisis." This crisis typically occurs in 30 and 40-year olds who compare what they *have done* with their lives to what they had *wanted to do*. They experience regrets as they suddenly realize that they chose to pursue distractions (e.g., incompatible relationships, material things that created large debts) that caused them to run out of the time necessary to achieve some of their goals. Just as people cannot bake a cake in half of the expected time by doubling the baking temperature, people also will not reach many goals if they delay pursuing them, even if they double their efforts later. *Life* is not a dress rehearsal. There are no second chances to relive your 20s with a better plan.

We begin a more thorough consideration of our essence across time by seeing how time integrates with relationships, and then apply similar insights to our money control. As an advanced exploration, we will then combine money, relationships, and time into a few possible courses of action.

(Incidentally, philosophy puzzles such as *The Autoscop* can help us to understand who we are and for what we stand. Philosophers such as Robert Nozick offer us insights into such questions within his book *Philosophical Explanations*.)

How We Can Use Time to Choose Better Relationship Partners

Previously, in the *Relationships* chapter, we noted how there was a *range of quality* associated with any characteristic, phenomenon, or group of people. With regard to people, we typically want to join with high quality people, whether they are our work colleagues or romantic partners (more on high quality and success in a moment). We will focus on romantic partnerships during this chapter. As we explore this type of relationship, you will probably notice that many of these same methods of analysis could also be applied to your non-romantic relationships.

As we saw with the attraction section of *Relationships*, if people only use their F.L.Y.— A.S.I.A. criteria when selecting romance partners, then they are only using the most primitive part of their relationship abilities, and they will have greater difficulty uncovering their potential partner's essence. For example, if a person claims to be smart, calm, and soulful during a dinner date, would anyone really be able to fully believe such a description unless they witness such behaviors from that person during a challenging experience? Even with higher level observations, learning a person's character takes time.

Using the neo-cortex portion of our brain, we can form higher-level analysis techniques that will make our relationships more human and stack the odds of a successful partnership in our favor. We have already developed the S.U.M.A. love model for evaluating our relationships. Now, using time, we can apply another view.

Statistics have shown that those who get married later in life (25 and older) are more likely to stay married. Why? One very plausible answer appears to be that older people have developed a better understanding of themselves—their essence—and therefore have a better idea of the type of person that would be a compatible partner for them. As a simple, personal essence assessment, how easily could you answer these five questions:

1. Who, or what, inspires you?

2. Who, or what, makes you mad?

3. How would you role-play "If I were in charge" (e.g., boss, teacher, President) during a big event that required decision-making (e.g., who to temporarily lay off, how to grade a paper, whether or not to go to war)?

4. What do you regret the most about some previous decisions that you have made?

5. What do your long-term, growth goals say about you (i.e., "By the time that I am 35, I want to have achieved...")? Are there any common patterns?

The preceding five questions help us uncover our essence by using different viewpoints. The first question is somewhat obvious. It asks you about role models and settings that lead you to act in a certain manner. It helps uncover what motivates you to take action.

The second question is a little less obvious. By considering what makes you mad, you are indirectly articulating your beliefs about fairness and injustice.

The third exercise of role-playing will help reveal what you value as most important during big events that require a decision. Sometimes, imagining how you would walk a mile in someone else's shoes reveals the differences that you perceive between them and you (in this case, someone who is in charge).

The fourth question allows you to prioritize any regrets and opportunity costs associated with your earlier decisions. You once made choices between competing priorities, but what did they cost you? Would you do any of those decisions differently, knowing what you now know?

Finally, the fifth exercise challenges you to consider what your priorities will be as a 35 year-old (or older, choose your age). You may go even farther with this fifth question and imagine what you would like people to say about you at your funeral. Alternatively, you might consider developing a motto or a quote that you would want written on your tombstone, reflecting your identity over time. What would those words be? Why?

All five of these questions help reveal your essence, and as your answers become more consistent over time, your essence becomes more evident. Of course, these questions also work well for gaining insight into somebody else's fundamental character, such as the essence of a potential romantic partner.

Just as greater self-knowledge appears to equip older people with an ability to find better matching partners, further evidence of the benefits of self-knowledge can be found by noting that successful businesses have also used an essence-based approach to develop their relationships. Each year, businesses spend millions of dollars to select the "best fitting" employees and business partnerships that will advance the company's essence—its mission and its values. Before businesses hire a new person or accept a new partnership, the potential new relationship must demonstrate at least two qualities:

1) The new relationship offers "something"—knowledge, skills, or abilities—that will grow the company.

2) The new relationship offers this "something" more effectively than other potential relationships.

Companies will review resumes and interview people to find that "something" within a person. We may also use higher-level, interview-like processes to find a good partner. One such process of analysis—"ScISSoRS"—allows us to cut away distracting F.L.Y.—A.S.I.A. urges and explore higher-level compatibility factors. "ScISSoRS" is an easy way to remember a partner analysis model that uses words beginning with the letters "S," "I," and "R."

Using "ScISSoRS" Information to Cut Through our Primitive Urges.

As you begin evaluating a current, or potential, romantic relationship, one of the first "S" factors that you should consider is the potential for *security*. Security distinguishes strong partnerships—particularly good marriages—from other types of relationships. Humankind's historical development reflects that people voluntarily enter into "social contracts" with others because they believe that it will make them more secure. For example, people support a government when it makes them feel more secure, via police, firefighters, and a justice system. In exchange for this safety, people willingly pay a price in terms of taxes and reduced personal liberties (i.e., I cannot drive my vehicle 90 m.p.h., but neither can anyone else, and we are all safer because of these laws). Similarly, in our romantic relationships we should be able to enjoy security as we share our greatest and most difficult times with each other.

In contrast, other relationships, such as our less intense friendships, might pledge to help us if we ever fall unto hard times, yet these people rarely pledge to place our security higher than anyone else's. If these (non-romantic) friends were to move away from us to pursue their personal goals, we would most likely say "good luck" to them, and not feel betrayed. We have a stronger expectation to feel safe, and to feel like a major priority of another person's life, when it comes to our intense romantic relationships. A few questions that you might ask about your relationship(s) after a period of time (particularly if you are considering marriage) could include:

Do you feel physically secure? Sexually pressured? Constantly compared to others?

Do you feel that you could tell your partner a secret and not worry about it being repeated?

Can you share your dreams, fears, or mistakes, without being ridiculed in return?

The next significant letter in the "ScISSoRS" insight model is "I," which stands for *individuality*. A person should not feel smothered as a result of a relationship. There should still be room for individual growth. The individuality can be subtle. For example, when some couples first start watching movies together, or rent videos together, they are inclined to watch something that both of them would definitely enjoy. This kind of constraint, while courteous, can also inhibit a person's growth. Instead of them always looking for a movie that they think both of them will like equally, couples might consider alternating between a movie that she really likes, and then a movie that they both equally like, and then a movie that he really likes. That way, both people still get to pursue their own interests, as well as expand their own minds while they learn more about their partner's essence. Questions of individuality might include:

Do you have interests that you like to do only by yourself?

Do you feel that you can pursue your own interests?

How much are you willing to sacrifice your own interests for the sake of your partner?

How could you share a part of your interests with others?

A pair of "S" words follows the "I"—*synergy* and *serendipity*. People achieve *synergy* whenever they create something greater together than they would have created through their individual efforts. For example, an interactive group of people exchanging ideas often produces a greater collection of wisdom than if the individuals independently listed their ideas separately on their own sheets of paper and then handed those papers to a group leader for tallying. Synergies may also be practical in nature, such as when married couples save money by sharing a car and living space. *Serendipity* refers to the spontaneous good things that can occur simply by being involved with high quality partners, mentors, or groups. With more high quality views and mindsets to draw upon, serendipitous moments are more likely to appear, such as when people help each other with their *Life* plans. A few serendipity and synergy analysis questions might be:

Do conversations with your partner usually lead to a better idea than you would have reached on your own?

How would your partner's core competencies compliment your core competencies?

Do you laugh together? Do you almost always have a good time together?

The "R" of ScISSoRS is *reciprocity*. As we attempt our goals, we expect to be supported by our relationships. At the same time, our partners have the right to expect us to provide them support as they pursue their goals. We should be willing to offer as many resources to others as we are hoping to gain from them. I have known work-aholics who complain about wanting a supportive partner, but they themselves would not be willing to cut back on their work, or their hobbies, to support another person. You cannot ask for more than you would be willing to offer.

This principle of *reciprocal support* can greatly complicate our ability to get things done, especially if many people need our support at the same time. We do not want to spread ourselves so thin in supporting others that we cannot achieve our own goals. Thus, we must prioritize our level of interaction and intensity with people. Typically, people prioritize their romantic partners as their biggest commitment for reciprocity. Have you?

Reciprocity also warns us to beware of people who have stayed in the "comfort" of an unsatisfying relationship while they looked for a new partner. These deceivers never had the courage to tell their current partner that they wanted to end the relationship. Instead, they hid their discontent and looked to "trade up" with a new person. Suppose that one of these "trade up" people approaches you with an offer to participate in an intensified relationship with them. Suppose further that, aside from their status of being in a relationship with someone else, this person appears to be precisely what you want in a partner. You must be very cautious about joining such a person who promises to break up with their present partner if you will join them. Remember, if they would <u>do</u> it <u>for</u> <u>you,</u> then they will likely later <u>do</u> it <u>to</u> <u>you</u> and reciprocate the pain that you (unintentionally) caused someone else! Some potential reciprocity questions include:

What do you offer your partner? What do you ask for?

What does your partner typically offer? What does your partner typically ask for?

Do you give as much as you receive?

A final "S" to look for in a partner is the quality of *success*. More specifically, has your romantic interest demonstrated the three characteristics associated with success—excellence, consistency, and intentionality? These characteristics deserve a bit more elaboration.

Excellent performance builds a foundation for top-notch, successful results. Yet excellent performance is not enough for success. Anyone can be lucky once or twice with their performance. For example, consider the gamesmanship associated with people "putting on their best image" during a first date. Anyone can pretend to be extremely polite or considerate for a date or two. Rather than falling "head over heels" for someone after a first date, graduates may wish to analyze their partner for <u>consistently</u> <u>excellent</u> behavior across multiple encounters.

As a third check of success, you may look for the "intention" behind someone's actions. A good outward image may not accurately reflect their inner essence. Consider, for example, how some athletes are naturally gifted. As a result, early in their sports endeavors they perform better than their peers with little effort. This can create laziness. The athletic "stars" might not strive to improve themselves, believing that they only need to be better than their peers in order to gain admiration. This mentality falls short of the principle of "growth," and reduces the star's chance of feeling lasting fulfillment and happiness. With intention, a person strives to give their best and improve, regardless of their current standing among their peers. A non-athletic example of intentionality would be the work effort that people display. Do they seek to be high quality contributors, or simply coast through their days performing just enough work to avoid being fired? Success questions that you might consider asking about someone include:

How has your partner demonstrated success? In their job? School? Sports?

Has the partner been consistently successful in one, or many, areas?

Has their success been intentionally grown, or was it due to luck...perhaps due to a lack of strong competition?

As suggested earlier, the "ScISSoRS" factors also allow us to evaluate the F.L.Y.—A.S.I.A. qualities of our partner as well. For example, the success factors may be applied in the following manner:

Did your partner earn her or his status (A.S.I.A.), or did she or he inherit it?

Is your partner's body "look" (F.L.Y.) due to fitness, or because of bad behaviors such as bulimia or smoking?

Is your partner intelligent (A.S.I.A.), or just a repeater of clever words that they heard elsewhere?

Thus, the "ScISSoRS" model helps us to uncover the essence of our partner and our relationship beyond the F.L.Y.—A.S.I.A. level. This longer-term, deeper view is necessary because people change over time and you want to uncover their most probable behaviors. For example, it can be riskier to commit to marrying someone who has just graduated from school, compared to someone who has been working full-time for a year or two at their job. The "new worker" risk is that you cannot be as certain about the kind of careerist your partner will be. New workers have not yet shown a consistent essence that predicts if they will prefer to work 40 hours per week, or 70 hours per week. Each type of careerist offers you advantages and disadvantages, such as more time or more money to spend together. After observing your partner's work habits over time (3 months? 1 year?), you will have gained a longer record of your partner's behaviors and can better predict if your lives can comfortably blend together.

If you do find someone worthy of your commitment, then you might consider discussing whether or not you wish to become wealthy as a couple. We explore this choice next.

If You Commit to Growing Wealthy...

Suppose that you have decided to commit to becoming wealthy—retiring from the need to work a 40+ hour-per-week job. Whether as an individual, or as a partner in a relationship, how will you determine what this particular level of wealth should be? Choosing how much money you might need can be aided greatly by using the often misunderstood tool known as a "budget." Too many people think that using a budget to plan their money is like using a diet to starve themselves from enjoying food. Budgeting, however, should not be about financial starvation! When properly done, a budgeting plan tells us where we are headed, instead of just where we have been. It opens up a new awareness of ourselves and how we prefer to use our money.

Budgeting focuses our money control. It also displays the effectiveness of our previous plans by measuring how well we have advanced toward our money goals. With a budget, we are able to see when we have traded away some of our goal-oriented control for other distractions. For example, with a budget we can see if we have spent more money each week on clothes or bar tabs, instead of investments or charitable donations. Businesses successfully develop their companies by using money management practices. Companies designate financial officers and accounting departments to monitor and analyze their company's "cash flow." Using this business-like perspective will allow us to focus our money controls and turn our goals into realities.

A simple, paycheck-to-paycheck budget technique follows. Since I believe in practicing what I preach, I offer you my family's budget from back in the year 2000. At that time, my "family" was composed of only my wife Karin and myself—not even any pets yet. We were in our late 20s and together earned around $55,000 a year (before taxes). At that time, we were focused on retiring from "necessary" work by age 50. Although your goals and destinations in your 20s will certainly differ from ours, the following pencil and paper budgeting method can work for any income level (although there are also a number of budgeting software packages that you could use, such as *Quicken* or *SmartBooks*).

The following budget displays our previous plan and use of our money. Since it is from the year 2000, prices were slightly cheaper than they are currently. Although this budget is designed to show you how we focused our money, versus the cost of items, if you really want to know what the dollar amounts from the year 2000 would be in more recent dollars, multiplying any of the values on page 84 by 1.2 would give you their approximate cost in 2012 dollars.

Pay Day, June 15th

1,760	Take Home Pay		(After deductions for taxes
-1,000	Investments		& insurance program)
760	Deposited to Checking Account...recorded on Check #573		
		Before / After	
-245	Rent	$245 / 490	(Not a palace, yet...)
515		- 490	Check #579
		0	
			(Car and Renter's / Apartment
-40	Insurance	$200 / 240	Insurance)
475			
-8	Cable TV	$16 / 24	(Basic cable)
467			
-8	Utilities	$15 / 23	(Water and Electricity)
459			
-45	Phone	$21 / 66	(Shop around for good rates)
414			
-25	Car Maintenance	$59 / 84	(Oil changes, tune ups,
389			yearly registration)
-30	Christmas	$320 / 350	(Set aside the money early)
359			
-30	Wedding	$300 / 330	(Many friends getting married)
329			
-35	Husband Fund	$7 / 42	(Personal Spending Money)
294			
-35	Wife Fund	$83 / 118	(Personal Spending Money)
259	For use on food, gas, Church, entertainment,		
	including clubs such as Phi Beta Kappa		

84

Yes, it was this simple to keep track of $55,000 every year. We created a new budget approximately every two weeks as we received our paychecks on the 1st and 15th of each month. No computers were necessary. It required a time commitment of approximately half an hour each week. We would start by writing down our take-home pay (the pay after taxes and other deductions, such as the deduction of a retirement plan, or an insurance plan). Then we would subtract what we anticipated spending on each budget priority during that two week period. During the above pay period, our "Take Home Pay" was $1,760.

The mechanics of this budget were rather simple. For this budget of June 15th, after allocating $1,000 to "Investments," we had $760 remaining. We then set aside $245 as half of the "Rent" payment (paid at the end of the month). We added that half-rent amount of $245 to the "Before" column of "Rent," which was the balance of the "Rent" category from the June 1st. This created a new "After" balance of "$490."

We then returned to subtracting money for each budget category from the left column, and added those amounts to each category's "Before" values, updating the "After" columns accordingly.

With the new balances established, we could then pay our bills. For example, on June 30th, we wrote a check for $490 to our apartment manager. We subtracted that money from our checkbook. We then subtracted $490 from the "After" column, which brought the "Rent" balance to "$0." Lastly, we wrote down the check number (#579) that we used to pay the rent on the budget sheet, as an extra bookkeeping measure. Later, when a new budget would be made for July, the "Before" column of "Rent" would contain a "$0." The updating would then continue as $245 would be allocated from the July 1st paycheck, giving the "After" column a balance of "$245."

The dollar values associated with each allocation revealed our focus for our money. So did the order of our allocation categories. For example, the first category for which we allocated our money was our top priority— investing as much as reasonably possible. We were not precisely certain about what standard of living we wanted to achieve back then, but we did know that we would need to save a good amount of money since we were a little older (our mid 20s) when we started investing. Since we did not want to "have to work" for the rest of our lives, we made investing our first priority, and then adjusted the rest of our priorities accordingly.

After our investments, our next biggest money allocation was housing. During that year, we chose to live in an 800-square foot apartment. It was small and simple, but more than adequate. We wanted to avoid the major opportunity costs that might have come from buying a home that was larger than we needed. Since we made over $50,000 a year (before taxes) and had no debts, we could have easily qualified for a home mortgage loan of at least $100,000. However, we had no children back then and wished to spend our non-work time doing things other than mowing a lawn or vacuuming extra large rooms. Living in a smaller apartment also allowed us to resist the urge to fill our dwelling with furniture that would be as classy—and expensive—as our parents. Additionally, we had heard that it took an "average" of four years before you could sell a house profitably. Since we were only going to live in the area for two years, we decided to rent, instead of own, our housing.

Our consideration of opportunity costs of housing space reflected our desire to avoid having too much "excess capacity." Excess capacity results from having more than we need. For example, suppose that we had enough furniture (a bed, couch, table, and two lamps) to comfortably fill an 800 square foot apartment. If we rented two 800 square foot apartments, but lived in only one of them, many people would call us "wasteful," if not "insane." However, if we had a single 1,600 square foot apartment, some people would have misguidedly called us "successful." Even though we would have been living well beyond our needs, some people would have been dazzled by our big apartment. We did not feel, back then, that the extra 800 square feet of unnecessary space was worth the extra money. We would have rather invested. So, instead of paying for a 1,600 square foot home, and therefore paying for 800 square feet of excess space, we added the saved difference to our investments.

Viewed as an opportunity cost, you can see that if Karin and I had taken a home loan with a $1,000 monthly payment, the actual monthly cost of the house would not have been just $1,000 a month. There would also have been an opportunity cost of the $510 difference ($1000-$490 current rent=$510) that we could have no longer invested. Additionally, the interest that we would have gained from that invested $510 needed to be considered as well, and that could be quite substantial over time.

These, of course, were our choices for our money, time, and relationships. If asked today, I could probably make a good argument for why Karin and I could have opted to buy a home—such as if "privacy" and "quiet" had been our highest priority. I recall a few times when it was after 10 p.m. and I had to knock on a neighbor's door and ask them to turn down their music (Karin's hospital work required waking up at 4:30 a.m.). Other reasons for home ownership include the pride that a person receives from having their own home. There are also certain tax advantages from home ownership, as well as the potential for the value of the property to increase over time, or the option to rent the home when you move to another location. For Karin and I, we decided that we would wait to find our "happily ever after" home until later, and so we viewed our lifestyle as "temporary" while we invested for bigger, future goals. We were comfortable making these choices because we were focused on certain destinations, and their costs, and we chose to use our *Life* controls accordingly.

Our next set of budget allocations paid the basic bills. Car insurance was necessary, and we also needed renter's insurance to cover our possessions within our apartment. Our utility expenses were only electricity and water, and our garbage service was included within the rent price. We typically had a phone bill of $70-$90—and that was without cell phones.

The other allocations were for future expenditures. We set aside money for car maintenance, which was usually an oil change every three or five months. We also set aside money for wedding gifts and travels—many of our friends became married during their 20s. Lastly, we set aside money for Christmas gifts. You know that holiday expenses will be coming, so you might as well plan for them in your budget, instead of paying off your credit card later—with interest.

Two other categories remain to be described. We established them in our budget because traditional folklore suggested that the top three reasons people divorce are related to arguments over money, religion and politics. To help control for the money issues, Karin and I agreed to the general budget priorities, and then received a personal allowance, or a "personal fund," to spend however we wanted during that period, or to save and carry over into the next pay period. By allocating personal allowances, I could spend $70 each month pursuing martial arts knowledge without Karin becoming frustrated by my "always spending money." Meanwhile, Karin could choose to indulge her artistic tastes and buy $200 worth of artwork every three months and I would never get concerned about her occasionally spending large sums of money in unpredictable ways.

Finally, at the end of the budget, did you notice how much was left over at the end of each paycheck? Karin and I used to have food allowances of $25 for each week. There were a lot of cereal, noodle, and vegetable meals back then…beans and rice came in handy as well. We would look for coupons in the local newspapers. Occasionally, we would playfully compete with one another to see who could eat better on a weekly allowance of $25. Although you may not wish to go to these levels of effort to save money, the main point of this discussion is simply to note that a large amount of savings can occur from intelligent food choices and purchases.

Our <u>lack</u> of certain budget categories also reflected some of our quantifiable choices. No money was used on car loans, school loans, or credit card payments, because we took our first years after college to pay off our debts and we did not want to endure those debt challenges again. Here is where our personal preferences guided us. Statistically speaking, the most likely "optimal" strategy with regard to car loans and student loans (both were under a 4% interest rate) would have been to pay them off as slowly as possible, keeping the maximum amount of our money in our stock market investments, where the expected long-term return would probably have been around 7%. However, we wanted to be stress-free if I had decided to change careers. Since we wanted to avoid having debt hanging over our heads, we opted to pay off our loans first.

Also, for five of the first ten years of our marriage, Karin and I were able to choose an apartment that was close enough to one of our places of work so that one of us could bike to work. By being a one-car family, we were able to save a great deal of money by not having a second car's worth of payments, insurance, oil changes, maintenance, and yearly license and registration fees. There were a few times when the opportunity cost of only using one car was the inconvenience of having to plan out our week's travels in advance, but this seemed to pale in comparison to the extra money that we were able to set aside for investing.

Lacking certain expenses, we were able to reduce our excess capacity and opportunity costs. Whether from a job, investments, or inheritance, approximately 15-25% of our income will eventually be taken from us in the form of taxes and deductions. When we *save* that money, however, we get to keep it all. Saving, whether by paying less, using discount coupons, or temporarily going without some wants, grows our wealth without the traditional deductions that accompany earnings. Since every dollar saved is worth more than every dollar earned (after considering taxes), being able to save on the automobile portion of our budget was very useful.

Let us return to the destination of "wealthy." What was "wealthy" to Karin and I? According to the budget from this time period, "wealthy" would have been a large enough income from non-job sources (e.g., pensions, assets, or businesses) to maintain our standard of living. At that time, assuming that we did not invest any more, bringing in $1520 a month ($760 x 2)—after taxes—would have been what we needed from our investments in order to maintain our standard of living. Of course, we did not always want to live at that standard of living. We were optimistic that we would have the chance to be parents in the future, and expected that we would probably want to add another car, as well as move to larger housing to make it all work together comfortably for us. These changes to our lives would likely require more money.

Eight years later, our *Life* had changed significantly. We were now parents of some great kids, and had added newer, bigger vehicles, as well as acquired a house with lots of "excess capacity" so that there was plenty of play space. Our monthly budget sheets from the year 2008 often looked something like this:

Pay Day, September 15th

		Before / After	
3,439	Take Home Pay		(After taxes & insurance)
-500	Investments		(House upgrades, 529s)
2,939	Deposited to Checking Account...recorded on Check #573		
-920	Mortgage and HOA	$920 / 1840	(Home, HOA, Garbage)
2,039			
-180	4-Wheel Drive Vehicle	$180 / 360	("Blizzard capacity")
1,839			
-45	Insurance	$110 / 155	(Car and jewelry)
1,794			
-100	TV + Phone + Internet	$100 / 200	("Communications")
1,694			
-155	Utilities	$15 / 170	(Water, Electricity, gas)
1,539			
-60	Christmas	$900 / 960	(More to shop for...)
1,479			
-100	Travels	$520 / $620	(Family vacation, return to grandparents)
1,379			
-125	Husband Personal Fund	$70 / 195	(Personal Money)
1,254			
-125	Wife Personal Fund	$255 / $280	(Personal Money)
1,129	(For use on food, gas, Church, and entertainment)		

(Entertainment included clubs such as Phi Beta Kappa and Mensa, & magazines such as *The Economist* and *Scientific American Mind*)

You can see how our use of our money control has evolved. Our top two money priorities are still the same—investments and housing. However, the amounts of money allocated to the priorities have changed. Notice how our investments are much smaller than they were eight years ago? (Pssst…kids can be expensive…they do not have to be…we just splurge a bit too much…)

Our investments have also changed in their type. We decided to diversify our investments more by improving our house, and placing less in the stock market, so that we could rent our house to others after we moved to our next location. We also created a "college savings plan" investment for our kids (see www.Savingforcollege.com for more information on 529s).

As for housing, our home mortgage included the cost of homeowner's insurance and the Home Owner's Association (HOA) fees that covered our garbage service.

We also added a four-wheel drive vehicle as our second vehicle, because we lived in Colorado. Although the four-wheel drive vehicle did not achieve the kind of gas mileage that we would have preferred, we wanted to have every chance to reach a hospital or grocery store in case of a blizzard. We viewed the expenses of poorer gas mileage as a form of "safety insurance."

With regard to the remaining funds, the categories did not change much, even if the values had. Our "leftover" funds at the end of the budget had become notably larger than they used to be, which was helpful because there were more now mouths to feed, clothe, and entertain. If we had been more serious about investing, we could have invested more, but we opted to enjoy more family vacations and other things that we often passed up during our 20s. As always, this is just one perspective on money. Your individual budgeting priorities may be completely different. As long as your budget reflects your goals, you are strengthening your essence.

Growing Money, Relationships, and Time Together

Whenever you are trying to develop an expectation of an outcome, it is often useful to consider some ideal circumstances and outcomes, and then scale back your expectations to more reasonable levels. Therefore, it seems worth exploring the rare, if almost impossible scenario, whereby two high school sweethearts are able to focus their controls toward growth almost immediately after graduation. For example, imagine that two people who previously lived in separate, $500-per-month apartments, decide to get married at the risky age of 19. At a minimum, they could move into a one-bedroom apartment together (if they decide to wait to produce children until their early 30s). From ages 19-28, the two of them would then be able to save $500 each month because one of them is no longer paying rent. If they invest that $6,000 each year ($500 x12 months) in an investment that returned 5% after-tax (or perhaps 5% in a tax-free bond), then their extra money from their actions would be approximately:

Age	Amount Invested	Start of Year Balance	5% Interest	End of Year Total
19	$ 6,000	$ 6,000	$ 300	$ 6,300
20	$ 6,000	$ 12,300	$ 615	$ 12,915
21	$ 6,000	$ 18,915	$ 946	$ 19,861
22	$ 6,000	$ 25,861	$ 1,293	$ 27,154
23	$ 6,000	$ 33,154	$ 1,658	$ 34,811
24	$ 6,000	$ 40,811	$ 2,041	$ 42,852
25	$ 6,000	$ 48,852	$ 2,443	$ 51,295
26	$ 6,000	$ 57,295	$ 2,865	$ 60,159
27	$ 6,000	$ 66,159	$ 3,308	$ 69,467
28	$ 6,000	$ 75,467	$ 3,773	$ 79,241
29	$ 6,000	$ 85,241	$ 4,262	$ 89,503
30	$ 6,000	$ 95,503	$ 4,775	$ 100,278
31	$ -	$ 100,278	$ 5,014	$ 105,292
35	$ -	$ 121,888	$ 6,094	$ 127,983
40	$ -	$ 155,564	$ 7,778	$ 163,342
45	$ -	$ 198,543	$ 9,927	$ 208,471
50	$ -	$ 253,397	$ 12,670	$ 266,067
55	$ -	$ 323,406	$ 16,170	$ 339,577
60	$ -	$ 412,757	$ 20,638	$ 433,395
65	$ -	$ 526,795	$ 26,340	$ 553,134

Chart 4-1: Ideal $6,000 Savings

(Note: The couple must also consider the "inflation" of prices. For example: $300,000 right now may only buy you $200,000 worth of the same items 20 years from now, if the annual inflation rate is 3%...see how by looking at the "Foolish Calculators" at www.fool.com.)

As Chart 4-1 shows, this romantic partnership would be greatly aided in becoming wealthy by investing that previous rent money. If there is such a

92

thing as a "lucky couple," then this scenario shows that time favors those who know what they want, including what kind of person they want, and are able to find it. Success favors those who are prepared. Time favors those who have prepared their *Life* ship. Of course, you should not try to get married as a result of this scenario. As the evidence from divorce statistics suggests, earlier marriages are riskier.

Consider the tragedy, then, of single students who do not attend college, or a two-year technical school, and choose to not invest at all. Mostly because of ignorance, they do not believe that investing a small amount like $167 a month can lead them to significant wealth ($167 x 12 months = $2,000 IRA contribution…remember Chart 2-1 on page 21?). As a result, they invest nothing.

Even worse, instead of investing, some people go out and buy the most expensive clothes, cars, and housing that they can. These spending actions ignore investment strategies that would stack their odds toward a better future. We stand a much better chance of achieving wealth if we invest $167 a month ($41.75 per week x 4 weeks) than if we spend $42 each week in extravagant housing or unnecessarily expensive vehicle payments. Often, downsizing our excess capacity in a vehicle or housing to meet our needs instead of all of our immediate wants is a way to free up $167 a month.

However, some people will still choose to create "time overlaps" with their money behaviors. For instance, whenever people use a credit card to "buy" a pair of pants, they have not yet truly paid for the pants. Instead, they have taken out a short-term loan from the credit card company. If they require two months to pay off the credit card bill, and the pants are worn during that period, the credit users have created "time conflicts." In reality, they have paid *full price plus two months of interest charges* for a *used* pair of two-month-old pants. This type of money behavior inhibits growth.

Not all time overlaps from credit are bad. Occasionally, you may plan to temporarily surge your *Life* ship strong with one control at the expense of the others. For example, you may want to devote your 20s to excelling at your career and socializing less. Alternatively, you might choose to raise a family early, in your 20s. The energy demands of a family will reduce your chances to work as much as your peers. Therefore, your longer-working peers, who have no children, will be more likely to get more work done and advance their careers more rapidly than you during that time period. Of course, we are not living our lives simply to compare our outcomes with others, are we?

With each choice we make, we temporarily alter our lives in favor of a personal priority. If we have freely chosen these priorities, with a reasonable knowledge of the opportunity costs associated with them, then we will more comfortably live with the outcomes.

"Free Time" is Imaginary.

As you continue to combine planning across time with your knowledge of opportunity costs, you might begin to see that one of the great fallacies often spoken in our culture is the concept of "free time." Our time is not free. Especially when we are young, when we can take maximum advantage of time, such as through second jobs and investing, the concept of "free time" is poorly labeled. Every moment of our non-job or non-school time offers us a chance to advance toward our goals.

If those goals are purely financial, or based on getting promoted at work to a higher level of pay and responsibility, then our moments of "free time" come with the opportunity cost of not working the extra hours to develop our future. Every Sunday spent in front of a television watching sports represents an excess capacity of "free time" that costs us opportunities to improve our work projects. Every Saturday spent shopping could be invested in activities that lead to an early retirement, such as a weekend job.

Instead of "free time," think of it as "personal time." How are you investing it?

At the same time, we should consider allocating time to have fun and leave space to rest and recover as a part of our balanced lives. Doing "nothing" is sometimes a productive use of time. Physical fitness basics demonstrate how to balance growth with rest. For example:

Suppose that you wish to increase the power of your arms. You enter a weight room and, after estimating your energy level and time constraints, you pick up some hand weights and begin curling your forearms upwards. If you have chosen the correct weight, then your arms begin to feel warm and strong. You flex and relax in a firm, rhythmic motion, and after eight to twelve repetitions, you pause to let your muscles relax before beginning the next set of motions. If you feel strong, you might even challenge yourself by going a little beyond your normal capabilities.

When you finish the sets of exercise, you usually wait a day or two before repeating the same routine. This resting allows your muscles time to recover and build up from the earlier resistance and strain. You may even feel a little sore the next day. This mild soreness happily reminds you of the previous day's accomplishments.

By being able to accurately assess your strength abilities, even if reality is a little humbling at first (e.g., you used lighter weights, or needed more rest, than expected), you comfortably grow stronger. However, if you choose a weight that is too heavy, or begin to expect "too much too soon," your muscles and efforts strain from the very beginning. You grunt, groan, and jerk your body around to lift your weights. Incorrect assumptions about your ability can leave you struggling to advance. If you greatly exceed your muscles' abilities, you might even tear a muscle and set your development back farther than if you had never attempted the weightlifting challenge in the first place.

To prevent unnecessary exercise injuries, some weight lifters use a lighter, warm-up set of weights before taking on the heavier challenges. For that same reason, elite runners also warm up their legs with light jogging. They do not just start sprinting. We should follow their example and "warm up," as well as allow "rest and recover" periods, within our *Life* journey so that we will remain strong. Otherwise, if we try to achieve too much too quickly, we might become burned out and frustrated by our extreme efforts and outcomes that are not as grand as we expected.

*****

Thus far, we have discussed a number of analysis and planning methods for three controls of our *Life* ship. This multiple view approach has been quite intentional. After all, as Abraham Maslow opined, if you only have a hammer as your tool, then everything problem looks like a nail. Rather than trying to pound our way through *Life* using one incomplete perspective, we would like to be able to use multiple tools to build our ability to reach our goals.

To that end, even as we have explored various goals, we have yet to examine which of those goals are worthy of our efforts. We examine such *Values* next.

Additional Principles:

Essence
Delayed Gratification
"ScISSoRS"

For Further Reflection:

1) What do you think describes your "essence," even as your body has changed? Do you have a motto?

2) How did you answer:

a. Who, or what, inspires you?

b. Who, or what, makes you mad?

c. How would you role play "If I were in charge" during a big decision if you were the boss? If you were the teacher? The CEO?

d. What do you regret the most about previous decisions that you have had to make?

e. What do your long-term, growth goals say about you? Any common patterns?

…as a result, how would you describe your essence, in 5 sentences or less?

3) How would your current friends describe you? Would their descriptions be the same as the descriptions by your oldest friends?

4) Typically, most people would prioritize their romantic partners as their biggest investment. Have you? Why or why not (remembering that you do not have to be like "most people," so what are your own unique reasons)?

5) Create your own budget. Are you comfortable at your current standard of living, or do you anticipate needing more money in the future for kids, a house, or other goals? What will need to change?

6) Can your recall a time when procrastination / too much "free time" prevented someone you knew from achieving a goal? More optimistically, can you recall how someone built up their essence over time to achieve a goal?

7) Imagine that, in anticipation of marriage, you and your romantic partner start working out a budget. As you discuss the various categories, you notice that your partner wants a much larger personal allowance for each of you than you think is prudent. Would you:

    a) ...try to change their mind?

    b) ...accept their spending as a price of being in that relationship?

    c) ...end the relationship?

For Further Investigation:

Robert Nozick, *Philosophical Explanations*

Daniel Robinson, *Consciousness and Its Implications*, www.teach12.com

Daniel Goleman, *Emotional Intelligence*

Inflation websites: http://www.westegg.com/inflation/infl.cgi
                      http://mwhodges.home.att.net/inflation.htm

Children's 529 Education Plans, www.Savingforcollege.com

Phi Beta Kappa, www.pbk.org

Mensa, www.mensa.org

The Economist, www.economist.com

Scientific American Mind, www.sciam.com

Values: Engaging with Fire

"The Roots of Violence:
  Wealth without work,
    Pleasure without conscience,
      Knowledge without character,
        Commerce without morality,
          Worship without sacrifice,
            Politics without principles..." – Mohandas Gandhi

Consider this scenario: You are walking to a friend's house. As you walk around a street corner, you notice smoke coming from a nearby home. You then hear screams from that building, so you begin to run toward it. Once you are inside of the house, you see that two hallway doors are blocked, and fire is rapidly approaching both rooms. You hear three screaming voices, most likely children, coming from the first door. From the second door, you hear what sounds like one baby crying. You probably have enough time to unblock only one door. Which door will you unblock first?

Whenever I ask my students this gruesome question, the consensus that I usually receive, after some uncomfortable whispering, is that they would unblock the first door. Typically, they conclude that they would choose "the greatest good for the greatest number of people." This guiding premise, more formally known as the *Utilitarian* principle, leads people to choose the room with three children's voices.

I then offer my students a bit more information: "What if the baby behind that second door was your friend's baby brother?" Later, I ask, "What if it was your baby brother?"

Suddenly, as the decision becomes more personal, guiding values such as *Loyalty* and *Family* emerge. Although the choice remains between one life and three lives, for many people that one life becomes worth more than the other three. Now that you have been informed of this new identity information, which door would you choose to unblock? Why?

However you respond, your choice reflects your *values*. *Values* are our sense of right and wrong that influence our behavior. They are the steering mechanism of our *Life* ship, guiding the use of our *money, relationships,* and *time* controls.

Values are distinct from mere opinions. Consider the values of these people:

Socrates	Abraham Lincoln	Jesus Christ
Mohandas Gandhi	George Washington	Moses
Martin Luther King	Joan of Arc	Muhammad
King Leonidas & 300 Spartans	Davie Crockett & 200 Alamo defenders	

The people listed above were willing to die for their values and, in many cases, so were their followers.

The values supported by these individuals changed the course of history for their people, their nation, and often their world. Values can be that world-altering. For example, consider the long-term outcomes of two well-known societies from the period of 200 A.D. One society, the Roman Empire, looked quite dominant during that time. In contrast, a group of people that the Romans persecuted—Christians—looked rather weak. However, as time passed, the Roman value system suffered from internal power struggles and external invaders. At the same time, the Christian community grew largely around a common set of values. 1,800 years later, it is unusual to find a toga-wearing Latin speaker, but it is rather common to be able to find a Bible in a hotel, bookstore, or home. By way of quiet evolution, or radical revolution, values can lead to world-altering outcomes.

Who Made You A Judge?

Have you ever been encountered a "know it all" person who has tried to force their opinions upon you and make you believe what they believed? Or have you ever experienced someone who listened to one of your ideas and then said "That's stupid"? Such experiences can leave us with an unflattering view of people who express opinions, especially negative ones. The experiences might also make us prefer to avoid stating negative judgments about other people. Our actions would follow the advice of "judge not, lest ye be judged"—advice that has been with us for over 2,000 years. Besides that advice being a nice example of the principle of *reciprocity*, it warns us against expressing our opinion about an action or behavior.

Or does it? How would this advice have been applied to the fans of Civil War hero, and later President, Ulysses S. Grant? By some estimates, admiring fans sent Grant over 10,000 cigars, further encouraging his habit of smoking cigars. Grant later died of throat cancer, which was most likely caused from his smoking habit. If the admirers of Grant had known about the negative effects from smoking, would they still have sent him those cigars? A person's good intention to support someone's "happiness habit," without a judgment of that habit's outcomes, can be deadly.

Of course, if you dare to develop your value system, and even test it a time or two by asking or debating issues with friends or strangers, then you should be prepared to receive the same type of consequences that would occur if you played with fire—burns (resulting from disgruntled relationships). Some people might stop talking to you, because they will think that you are a trouble-maker ("How dare you disagree!", "Why do you want to rock the boat?!?"). Other people, who disagree with you, may label you as an "ignorant, _____ hater" (fill in your term: religion, minority, liberty, etc.). Differences in values between too many people can even lead to violence, as was the case in America's Revolutionary War, as well as its Civil War.

Occasionally, some people will appreciate that you offer them an alternative point of view, but there will also be "know it alls" who will react defensively to any differences in perspectives. When discussing value-rich topics such as money, religion, and politics, it seems inevitable that differences will emerge. Indeed, it is likely that some of the perspectives that people read within this *Life* book will be different—possibly irritatingly different—from some of their current beliefs.

Yet if people choose to keep quiet about their values and do not even think through an issue, then they will be subject to society's peer pressures. These peers and their values can reduce a person's outcomes and happiness. Studies have shown that college students' study habits can be negatively affected by peers (roommates) who play too many video games or have a drinking problem. This research warns us that as we choose the values that we will align our *Life* with, we must also be willing to look at our peer relationships for how they support or degrade our values.

As our intelligence improves, we will be able to look and choose peers who have demonstrated the value of "quality growth" (intentional, consistent, excellence) within their *Life*. These types of peers allow us to calmly compare differences among each others' viewpoints—as Scientists—and learn new insights that improve each other's *Life* performance. Such a peer group does not guarantee that we will always agree with each other, but our civil discussions will probably produce more useful ideas than a series of one-sided, pushy Lawyer exchanges.

One way that you may gain people's support, or animosity, for your beliefs—without aggressive, Lawyer speeches—is by the outcomes associated with your life. More specifically, if people claim to follow a certain set of values, and these people are typically miserable and non-productive with their lives, then their value system does not appear attractive to outside observers. Alternatively, if a group of people can articulate the values and principles that have guided their actions, and they are generally content and productive with their lives, then their value system is more likely to be respected by onlookers. Actions, and outcomes, do speak louder than words.

Of course, claiming to follow a code of values and actually following that code can be two unrelated actions. As a priest once told me, "The greatest risks to organized religion are religious people." The priest then explained to me that when people claim to be religious, yet do anti-religious actions—such as using illegal drugs or engaging in extra-marital sexual affairs—they break with religious values while at the same time confuse some non-religious people into thinking that such degenerative behavior is typical of religious people. When religious leaders such as Jim Bakker are exposed for their immoral financial dealings and extra-marital affairs, then religion's ability to be viewed as "a guide for living your life" becomes weakened.

Thus, the "judge not, lest ye be judged" advice should be noted for what it is—advice. It is not a prohibition on developing judgments. Instead, it is a call for the principle of *role modeling* the behaviors that you believe and for you to show that those behaviors lead to positive outcomes. Anyone can judge and criticize someone, but those who want their judgments to be considered seriously will be need to be role modelers of growth and productivity. These role modelers and judges can expect to be scrutinized by those who disagree with their views.

A classic American role model is General George Washington, who believed enough in America's Revolution for Independence that he was willing to command its Continental Army. Moreover, he was willing to ride to the front battle lines between the American and British forces, often under fire, so that he could better direct the movements of the American forces. His living example that "these values are worth fighting for" was a major reason that his troops were willing to follow him and fight. After the war, his soldiers were even willing to fight for him to become a type of king and benevolent dictator. This new status would have allowed Washington to wield power and quickly resolve issues, such as finally paying some of the Continental soldiers for their wartime service. Yet Washington promptly rejected this king-like offer from his soldiers, and even retired from the Army. This type of "I serve for the good of all, not just myself" role modeling was a major reason that he was later trusted with the honored position of America's first President. Similarly, the role modelers listed on page 99 were able to inspire their followers to live a certain set of values and do great things.

It can be difficult to achieve Washington's level of role modeling (then again, he did own slaves…See? There is that scrutiny that comes along with being a role model…). Some people do not take time to reflect upon their values, and consequently are not able to explain them or role model a consistent system for others. Even when people do know how they want to live, unexpected pressures can affect the role modeling of their values. For example, consider the results from an experiment by researchers John Darley and Daniel Batson. They conducted what has become known as "The Good Samaritan Experiment."

John and Daniel studied a group of theology students who were preparing short speeches on religious topics. The students were separately told to leave their current room and go to another building to present their speeches. Some of the students were also told that they needed to hurry because they were late. During each student's short journey between the buildings, the students encountered a slumped-over man—an actor who, unknown to the students, had been asked to act in that slumped-over manner. The researchers then observed if the theology students diverted from their travels to help the pre-positioned, "sick" man. The results showed that those students who were in the biggest hurry were the least likely to help. The "hurry up" pressure was enough to cause the students—who were committed to studying religion and were engaged in a religious task—to act in a non-religious, self-centered manner. This research warns us that we must be cautious about our busy lives and hurried attitudes leading us to lose control of our time and, even more importantly, our values. A modern day, humorous re-test of "The Good Samaritan Experiment" can be found in the first season of the Sci-Fi Channel's reality series *Who wants to be a Superhero?*

In an attempt to become good modelers of our values, we will use this chapter to consider values that will improve our understanding of people's behaviors as well as increase our ability to live a more fulfilling life.

Competing, Fiery Value Biases

If we want to discuss *Life-altering values* as a Scientist, rather than as a Lawyer, then we must understand the assumptions associated with the ideas that any person puts forth. Once we understand a person's value biases, we may then better predict their choices and their resulting actions. Such an understanding allows us to create a more intelligent interaction with that person.

One way to uncover a person's biases is to ask them questions. For example, do you believe that killing a <u>caterpillar</u> is the same action as killing a <u>future</u> <u>butterfly</u>? If so, then your beliefs reflect what is more formally known as *Natural Law Philosophy*—a perspective that tries to understand and harmonize people's actions with nature's example of orderly development. In this case, the assumption that a future butterfly has been killed because a caterpillar has been killed reflects the value that a caterpillar will naturally grow into a butterfly.

By that same natural law perspective, then, an abortion of a fertilized human egg—a zygote—is the same as killing a future blastocyst, a future embryo, and a future human child. No matter what name a person calls the human organism during its development, at the moment of fertilization that organism possesses all of the DNA growth potential necessary to achieve the orderly advancement of a human life, including phases as a child, adult, and senior citizen. From a natural law perspective, then, most abortion procedures should be illegal because they are akin to the "murder" of an innocent human life.

In contrast, if someone uses the perspective of *Individual Liberty,* then the choice of abortion is a woman's fundamental right because it deals with her body, and hers alone—the status of the organism within her body is not the primary consideration. John Stuart Mill identified liberty as a person's freedom to act, as well as an absence of coercion upon that person's actions. If someone begins with an assumption of individual liberty as their highest priority, then a woman's access to an abortion should not be infringed upon by an "outsider" government law, or even medical science evidence.

Until people can agree that abortion is an issue of "rights" or "murder" (both highly emotional terms), an agreement about its correctness will not occur. The desire for an abortion and a person's view of a pregnancy can also be biased by one's current social status in life. For example, unmarried people (often teenagers and twenty-somethings) perceive pregnancy to be an unwanted "risk" that will interfere with their career plans. In contrast, married people who want children perceive this condition to be a "joy." I remember when, a few years after Karin and I were married, I was answering a medical health questionnaire for a doctor. One of the questions asked "Are you taking action to protect against pregnancy?" I would have understood if the question had asked if I were using birth control measures to "prevent pregnancy" (a more neutral, functional phrase), but not "protect against pregnancy." "Protect," a more emotive term, seemed to assume that my wife's fertilized eggs would be an attack upon my relationship and my livelihood. Perhaps if I had been single when I answered that questionnaire I would have not even noticed the choice of the word "protect" versus "prevent." My social status as a husband and my desire to be a father was biasing me.

Just as the act of an abortion can be viewed from the perspectives of natural law, individual liberty, or social status, the issue of "equality" can be viewed from multiple perspectives as well, such as *Equality of Opportunity* and *Equality of Result*. Those with an "equality of result" orientation are more inclined to support initiatives that lead to similar outcomes for all participants, regardless of the effort or risk that the more successful participants had to endure. For example, the United States tax code currently taxes the earnings of the wealthiest Americans more than the lowest earning Americans. Additionally, at the time of this writing, the rules of the United States tax code result in over 40 percent of Americans paying no taxes (typically the lowest income earners). Questions about whether this tax system is "equal" become major value issues during political elections. The Democrats are more likely to raise the taxes of the wealthier Americans, believing that the money should be used on programs that improve the odds of all citizens achieving some minimum income level. In contrast, the Republicans are more likely to lower the taxes on Americans, believing that lower taxes motivates people to achieve wealth, resulting in business growth and the creation of more jobs.

Those with an "equality of opportunity" perspective are also more likely to hold a "may the best person win" value bias. These types of people have sued colleges and universities for their "affirmative action" policies of accepting individuals with lower academic credentials and accomplishments even though more accomplished students were available for acceptance. Debates about affirmative action have been decided by the U.S. Supreme Court, including two University of Michigan cases that were decided in the year 2003. In general, the Court stated that a college may create a "diverse learning environment" through the acceptance of diverse applicants (not necessarily based only on academic accomplishment). However, the Court also stated that the college admissions programs were not allowed to create quota systems that guaranteed entrance to a specific number of "diverse environment" applicants. One of the Court opinions also suggested that affirmative action programs might no longer be needed by the year 2028.

Of course, the learning and training environments of schools differ greatly from the "win or lose" and "for profit" environments that require results-oriented competitions. Thus, sports teams do not use affirmative action values when they pick their team's players. Similarly, affirmative action requirements that would force lesser accomplished individuals to be hired over more accomplished individuals would likely reduce an organization's effectiveness. This value bias has been a voting issue. Since the 1990s, voters in states such as California, Washington, and Michigan have worked to end affirmative action programs at the state level. They have typically voted on value wordings such as:

"The state shall not discriminate against, or grant preferential treatment to, any individual or group on the basis of race, sex, color, ethnicity, or national origin in the operation of public employment, public education, or public contracting" (underline emphasis added). To see an interesting perspective on this particular voting act from a non-white male, consider reading Ward Connerly's *Creating Equal: My Fight Against Race Preferences*.

"Equality of opportunity" advocates gained further support for their "may the best person win" philosophy during the election year of 2008. During that year, the achievements of President Barack Obama, Presidential contender Hillary Clinton, and Vice Presidential candidate Sarah Palin showed how diverse Americans, and not just white males, were capable of earning America's top jobs without affirmative action programs. The 2008 election year may one day be remembered as a key moment when people reassessed whether there was a <u>need</u> for government programs to try and produce "equality."

Just as "equality" may be categorized and supported differently depending upon the environment, the issue of "respecting someone else's values" can also depend upon the surrounding circumstances. For example, imagine that a group of Western Europeans are hiking up the Himalayan Mountains when they encounter a young man sitting in the snow. The small, teenage-looking boy is covered with snow, and he looks sickly. The Europeans pick up the boy, and take him back to their camp. After he is fed warm soup and falls asleep for the night, he awakens in the warm tent full of fear and fury. The Europeans are confused—they thought that the boy would be grateful. What the Europeans did not know was that they had just interrupted the young man's three-day mountain "transition into manhood" ritual. The boy was supposed to have survived three days in the mountains with only minimal food. Although his judgment to accept help was weakened by his fasting, the boy will still be held accountable by his tribe for having failed his trial. Were the Europeans correct when they intervened?

Even if the Europeans had understood the local people's customs, would the Europeans have been correct to leave the boy alone when he looked as though he might die? Consider the closely related examples from the rare, but true, medical cases in the United States where children die because their parents favored using "prayer only" healing methods instead of traditional Western techniques (such as a shot of medicine). These scenarios prompt us to consider at what point a person's belief system, or a parents' belief system, has a greater correctness than an "outsider's"—such as a doctor's—opinion.

If you believe that somebody's values are only applicable in certain situations, then you are using assumptions aligned with *Moral Relativism*. This type of bias does not believe that there are absolute standards of right or wrong, but instead strongly considers the personal or cultural circumstances surrounding each event.

In contrast to moral relativists, there are the *Moral Absolutists* who believe that some standards do universally apply to all cultures at all times. For example, an absolutist would say that Hitler's war policies of abusing and extinguishing millions of Jewish people were wrong then, and would still be wrong today. Relative to their culture and rules of conduct, the German military of World War II behaved rationally and legally. Using a moral relativism bias, the concentration camps cannot be judged as "evil"—they were just a unique set of actions within the context of a war. Absolutists find this line of logic to be shameful. They would also cite scenarios involving rape, murder, and slavery as additional examples of behavior that should not be viewed "relatively."

The biases of natural law, individual liberty, equality of opportunity, equality of result, moral relativism, and moral absolutism are some of the biggest competing values that graduates will encounter throughout their *Life*. The next time you find yourself having a disagreement about somebody's words or actions, ask yourself, "What are my starting assumptions?" as well as "What are their starting assumptions?" If you can uncover these differences using a Scientist-like inquiry, then you will be well on your way to understanding someone's values. A strategy for uncovering the values of various relationship partners follows...

PIES: Common Personal Values

With all of the possible confusions and disagreements that can result from unknown biases, it would be useful if we could learn about others, and our relationships with others, using a common values model. Fortunately, the P.I.E.S. model offers you a relationship framework with four different views—Physical, Intellectual, Emotional, and Spiritual. P.I.E.S. allows you to ask others, such as friends or a romantic interest, questions about the values that they prioritize every day.

The four value realms of P.I.E.S. interact with each other. For example, suppose that someone says something that offends us. Our emotional irritation or anger with this person will be reflected in our physical realm through our increased blood pressure and heavier breathing. Our initial negative emotion might also cause us to intellectually develop an insult that we want to hurl at the person who offended us. This chain of reactions would satisfy our spirit of "revenge" that may temporarily be biasing us.

If, however, we are a bit more evolved, then our intellectual realm might remind us to restrain our emotionally driven urges. Intellectually, we might rationalize that if we did something cruel to our offender, then the confrontation may further escalate to more words, or even fists. At the same time, our spiritual inclination might be biased toward forgiving all first-time offenders—maybe, we might intellectually rationalize, "that person did not intend to offend us." This might then lead our intellect to look for the words to create peace with our offender, which would then cause our emotional tensions to fade, and would ease our physical blood pressure and breathing back to normal. Then, as a Scientist, we may explain to the person that they offended us, and then ask the person about the intent of their earlier words.

The previous scenario suggests that our P.I.E.S. realms might have the following hierarchy of dominance:

| Spiritual |
| Intellectual |
| Emotional |
| Physical |

Chart 5-1: The P.I.E.S. Hierarchy

Within Chart 5-1, the placement of the spiritual realm at the top reflects how the values composed within our spirit have the greatest guiding potential for our other realm responses. Chart 5-1 also has a building-block structure. This reflects that whenever any of the lower blocks are weakened, it is difficult to achieve optimum performance at the higher realms. For example, if we use extra energy studying or working overtime during a series of challenging weeks, we will probably miss some sleep at night and possibly become a little ill. Once we become physically tired and sick, we are more likely to find it emotionally difficult to be patient during frustrating situations, and we might snap at people over situations that would not ordinarily bother us. Regardless how intellectually quick or spiritually pleasant and forgiving we may ordinarily be, physical illness makes it tougher for us to be in harmony with our environment and our relationships. Weaker lower realms make it more challenging for us to achieve our higher realm capabilities.

This dominance-and-dependency order of the realms coincides with our maturity. Babies exemplify the lower realms during their earliest days of dependency. When they experience a physical discomfort, such as hunger, infants emotionally respond with crying or screams for someone else to fix their problem. As they grow older and learn greater independence, children intellectually learn to satisfy their hunger by going to the kitchen and acquiring some food. With greater maturity, their spirit might even incline them to think of others, and they may even offer to make a snack for others while they take care of their own needs.

The P.I.E.S. realms provide us with more insight into our romantic relationships. For example, people can examine their relationships to see if they have evolved beyond the physical appearances and physical resources of the F.L.Y.—A.S.I.A. model. Relationships should not be built solely upon physical F.L.Y.—A.S.I.A compatibility. Otherwise, either partner may be easily replaced whenever some other person offers similar physical substitutes. Physical realm traits are too shallow and superficial to be the only basis for a relationship—there are three other realms to consider!

At the same time, the dominance-and-dependency order suggests that the physical realm offers some very practical compatibility issues upon which to build. For example, if you enjoy exercising for two hours each day, finding someone with a similar fitness value might be a good idea. If you choose a drastically less fit partner than yourself, then your partner might eventually view you as a fanatical, restricted, "health nut" who spends too much of life's precious time in a "go nowhere gym." Alternatively, you might begin to perceive your less fit partner as weaker, lazier, or not respectful of the body that carries their soul. A major difference in your bias of what it means to be "fit" can be detrimental to your relationship. In contrast, similarly fit partners share a value that they can easily understand and support with one another.

Physical values can also be appreciated because they are rather easy to verify. In contrast, when people tell you about their spiritual values, such as by claiming that they are "patient and kind," you will have to wait until you see them tested with a controversial event before you can acquire credible evidence. Among the four realms, physical fitness seems to be the hardest to fake.

Notice that the word "fitness," versus "beautiful," was used. Some people maintain a fit-looking figure through unhealthy habits such fad dieting, smoking, or metabolism-altering drugs. Rather than focusing on shallow surface beauty, we should consider whether the fit appearance represents the spiritual values of excellence, consistency, and intentionality.

The next value realm for considering another person's compatibility is their emotional development. It can be challenging to categorize someone's general emotions into a level of maturity. It is difficult enough trying to understand simple emotive terms. For example, consider what happens when you are eating at a restaurant with some friends:

You ask your friends, "How was your meal?"

They respond, "It was good."

Their statement of "good" can be hard to categorize because there are so many positive words, such as "better than average," "nice," or "fine." We may need to use other references, such as the person's tone of voice, to guide us.

To overcome such confusions about "good," whenever Scientists try to analyze someone's reactions, they often use rating scales. Perhaps you have eaten at a restaurant, and received a receipt that included the opportunity to fill out an on-line survey. That restaurant survey likely asked you a question such as, "On a scale of 1 to 5, how much did you enjoy your meal?" A score of "5" would usually represent the best possible satisfaction that you, the customer, could feel. The confusions about a person's feelings are reduced when they are answered with numbers such as "3," "4," or "5." After restaurant researchers collect hundreds of responses from the surveys, they then use their statistical analysis methods to determine what distinguishes "good" from "great"—perhaps "good" is a "3," or possibly a "4."

However, we usually do not want to be quite so numerically analytical with our romantic partners, so we might consider other ways of measuring their emotional maturity. We can gain some insight by observing our partner's behavior whenever they encounter a challenge. Scale 5-2 offers one potential observation scale:

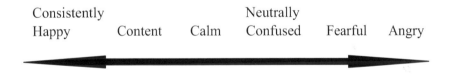

| Consistently | | | Neutrally | | |
| Happy | Content | Calm | Confused | Fearful | Angry |

Scale 5-2: Emotional Maturity Response

As Scale 5-2 shows, there are many possible responses to an adverse situation. Suppose that a person says something that offends their romantic partner. Would the partner's first response be anger? Some people will experience deeply negative feelings about their partners, such as anger or distrust, before they learn about their partner's reason for their statement or actions. People with this type of emotional reaction might wish to re-examine their biases and why they entered, or continued to remain, in their relationship. Such anger can burn out a relationship.

Alternatively, if people have confidence that their higher level abilities previously led them to select a good partner (perhaps they used a ScISSoRS-like selection process), then the worst emotion that they will feel is most likely confusion. Their spiritual and intellectual reaction to a controversial-looking situation might begin with the question, "Do I believe that my partner had my best interests in his/her heart and action?" If that answer is "Yes," then the belief that their partner had good intentions makes it is easier for the offended person to believe that their partner unintentionally made a mistake. The offended person may then calmly, like a Scientist, ask their partner about the reasons for their choice of words, or actions, as well as request an apology. Although we may be occasionally disappointed by our partner's actions (no one is perfect), our response to those disappointments reflects as much about ourselves as it does about our relationships.

This higher level, mature response also requires the use of our next value realm—intelligence. It can be hard to uncover our own, or another person's intelligence because we may each have our own premise of what it means to be intellectually "smart." There is no absolute, agreed upon scale for measuring or describing overall intelligence, although some scales of our intellectual ability can be found in grade point averages and test scores from knowledge assessments such as SATs, ACTs, GREs, and GMATs. Additionally, some I.Q. and cognitive ability tests have been shown to be reasonable predictors of a person's job performance abilities (for example, visit www.wonderlic.com).

Even though assessment scores can be perceived as "book smarts," we should remember that a person's poor grades, or test scores, do not necessarily mean that a person has not learned the material. Poor grades mean that someone did not *demonstrate to the grader* that they learned the material. Such a difference points out a key aspect of relationships between people—it is often not what we know, but how well we *communicate* what we know that matters most. People may only make informed decisions based upon the knowledge that is presented to them. Whether they are teachers judging homework, bosses evaluating employee performances, or you analyzing a romantic partner's actions and intent, you can only judge and predict based upon the information that you have received. For this and other reasons, we will explore the challenge of *Communication* in an upcoming chapter.

Information uncertainty about intelligence helps explain why, when people try to gain admission into a college, college entrance committees often require applicants to submit high school grade point averages and one of the standardized tests (ACT, SAT, etc.). While they are incomplete measures of a person, they are a quantifiable standard for initially comparing people. Since an "A" average from one school might have been easier to earn than an "A" average at another school, a standardized test provides a common way to compare applicants. College admission committees might also look at an applicant's club memberships and community service to learn more about them as a "whole person," but most selections start with some review of comparable intellect. Unfortunately, this measure is only part of intelligence.

The other part of intelligence remains elusive from those who attempt to measure it in strict, quantifiable terms. For example, have you ever met a "book smart" person who has a hard time interacting with people? They lack the other intelligence—"street smarts"—that helps people adapt and survive in various environments. "Street smarts" is also known as "common sense." "Common sense" is not that common. Otherwise, everyone would have it and no one would be upset over other people's lack of it.

An example of "street smarts" is the ability to interact well with a variety of people. This cannot be tested by standardized, formal exams. Its testing occurs when people interact across different environments, such as construction sites, beauty parlors, and university lectures. This "smarts" is highly valuable. For example, while researching millionaires, Thomas Stanley discovered that many of his millionaires did not have amazing standardized "book smart" test scores, but they were very skilled at being "street smart" personable. You can read more about these studies in Thomas's book, *The Millionaire Mind*.

Since there are two kinds of intelligence, and one kind cannot be quantified as well as the other, asking potential partners questions is one way of gaining insight into their intelligence. This is why companies often use interviews as part of their employee selection process for a job. Often, interviewers ask each applicant the same questions and later compare the answers. The answers may then be analyzed based upon the number of issues that each person considered, as well as how accurately the applicants predicted the outcomes from various hypothetical scenarios.

Similarly, although it is less emphasized as a part of the romantic adventure, partners may "interview" each other to uncover their "street smarts" intelligence compatibility. Observing a partner in multiple situations provides you some of this information. Asking them for their responses to various questions, such as the questions within this *Life* book, also provides you more information about their understanding of choices and outcomes.

You could also ask your trusted group of peers for questions that they like to ask their potential partners, and borrow the questions that seem most applicable to your situation. Such question and answer interactions help explore the intelligence realms of the P.I.E.S. compatibility system.

The final realm of compatibility is the spiritual realm. A person's spiritual character might be described as their broad philosophy for interacting with their world. For example, consider how a man might perceive a woman. If he uses only a narrow F.L.Y urge to view her, this will lead him to behave a certain way toward that woman. Alternatively, if he uses a different, spiritual value perception, such as "this is someone's daughter," or "she is my sister within the family of my God," this will produce a different set of behaviors. The spiritual perspective requires a cultivated mind, and not a response to urges. When Confucius demonstrated the "weeds outcome" from his uncultivated garden (in our first chapter), he was also demonstrating the effects from not cultivating one's self.

Some spiritual values can be learned rather easily. For example, asking a partner about their religion, or their lack of one, will reveal some aspects of their spiritual compatibility. However, we must be alert for spiritual value illusions. For example, just because we see someone go to a synagogue, church, or mosque during a weekend does not mean that he or she is any more spiritual than someone else. People may daydream through their entire religious service and come away with no more of a renewed spirit than if they had stayed at home.

Rather than relying upon someone's attendance at religious services, consider viewing a partner's spirit when they encounter challenges such as time crunches, opposing values, money troubles, or relationship difficulties. To paraphrase from the teachings of Socrates, a person's spiritual character is best represented by what they do when they think that no one else is watching them (see the section about "The Ring of Gyges" in Plato's book, *The Republic*).

In this section, we have looked at four common value realms for assessing relationships. Value questions that you might consider asking about your romantic relationship include:

1. How would you describe your value of fitness? Do you make it a priority? Does your partner?

2. When a troubling situation arises, can you respond calmly, like a Scientist? How about your partner?

3. Do you believe that you possess "book smarts," "street smarts," or both? What about your partner?

4. What value bias, religion, or attitudes (e.g., "optimist," "pessimist," etc.) best describes your guiding spirit? Your partner's?

What Is Worth Pursuing?

If reasonably intelligent people start with different beginning assumptions, then their differing values will often lead them to different conclusions. This can leave a Scientist disheartened, because it suggests that guiding values and ethics might just be relative to a certain person's perspective.

Fortunately, as we discussed at the outset of this book, there are intelligent ways to make choices and predict their outcomes, including with values. For example, if you encounter someone who claims to follow the relativist position of "whatever feels good, I do," then you can begin to study that person's actions and outcomes. If you have studied psychology, then you have probably encountered how humans typically desire to eat foods full of sugar, salt, and fat (most likely because it would have helped our ancient ancestors build up fat storage and survive the winter season). You can still feel the satisfaction of fulfilling these desires whenever you go to a restaurant and eat a fatty burger with salted fries while drinking a sugary soda or shake.

Alas, in today's modern world of climate control, we no longer "need" to have these urges influencing our eating behavior. Yet the urges remain, and as a result, the "if it tastes good, eat it" urge has led to approximately 50 percent of American adults being overweight or obese. Therefore, using the individual relativist value of "If it makes me feel good, I do it" as a guide for behavior appears to be dangerous. Such a value bias could also be used to justify a drug addiction behavior. It could even be used to justify a romantic relationship, because a person might have a feeling of "I have never felt this good with anyone else before." However, what if the relationship was only the mere satisfaction of lower-level, F.L.Y.—A.S.I.A. urges? Perhaps F.L.Y.—A.S.I.A. compatibility is better than no compatibility, but would you really want to risk a marriage on it?

Instead of relying upon limited personal urges, we might search for some consistent intellectual and spiritual guides that have resulted in happy lives throughout history. For example, if we examine the values that have been endorsed by generations of people for over 2,000 years, we will find at least one common question that has been asked:

The question that has been asked: *W*hat *C*an *M*ake *J*oy?

The above question uses a sentence to remember the four guiding values that serve as an answer:

*W*isdom, *C*ourage, *M*oderation, *J*ustice

These common values have been found throughout the world, in the teachings of Aristotle (Europe), Confucius (China), Lao Tzu (China), the *Bhagavad-Gita* (India), as well as monotheistic religions (Middle East). These common values emerged from societies that differed greatly in their cultural priorities. For example, Socrates and his Athenians citizens had a huge bias toward individual freedom, while Confucius's Chinese society was more concerned with collective order, and not individual freedom. Yet these distinct thinkers independently developed and defended the same basic values. That these values were selected by so many productive cultures and across so many time periods strengthens the case for why they are still values worthy of emulation today. These four values deserve a bit more elaboration.

Wisdom is reflected by our pursuit, and appropriate use, of intelligence. If we can develop an ability to predict what will happen in various situations, then we are more likely to obtain a joyful life. The second value, *courage,* is your ability to face what appears to be a difficult situation (it may turn out to be easier than you think). There will be many times in your life when you will face difficult-appearing situations. Although the situations will not always involve life or death decisions, they may involve you becoming unpopular to some people (due to your values). Courage is one of the four enduring values that will guide your continued support of those decisions. The next value, *moderation,* suggests that we should avoid extreme behaviors. Just as the *Time* chapter demonstrated how we need to incorporate rest periods into our physical fitness growth (or else we might burn out), we must also be cautious of exerting too much effort within too short of a time period in our other realms. Additionally, the guidance "All things in moderation—including moderation" also suggests that vacations or other recharging activities should be integrated into our routines to that we will be strong for our challenging periods of adventure. The fourth and final value of *justice* reminds us to act fairly, whether we are developing agreements, rewards, or punishments. For additional exploration into a more lasting fulfillment, consider reading Arthur Seligman's book, *Authentic Happiness.*

Together, behaving with wisdom, courage, moderation, and justice as we travel through life can help lead us to joyful outcomes, even if we are not completely certain about where we should go. If a person follows "The Golden Rule" of "Do unto others as you would want done unto you," then these four values appear to be good guides for how we "do" our actions. Immanuel Kant expressed a similar reciprocity "Golden Rule," arguing that a basis for judging an action is to ask (paraphrasing), "Would I be able to justify this type of action as an action that everyone in the universe should do?" For example, should everyone act "honestly," or "selfishly?" Each of these "do" value guides reflect a wisdom about reciprocity, as well as offer a guide for evaluating the actions of a potential partner—do they act with W.C.M.J. behaviors(?)…and of course, "Do I?"

Many of the key events in US history, from the Declaration of Independence to the Civil Rights movement, depended heavily upon rallying behind the W.C.M.J. values as reasons to fight for appropriate freedoms and equality. In contrast, there have been other nations throughout history that have lacked those standards for moral behavior. Lacking a moral authority, the main authority that such governments used was "physical power" and the ability to wield violence to crush those with opposing values.

Consider what would have happened to Ghandi, or Martin Luther King Jr., if they had tried their peaceful protests during Hitler's rule in Germany, or Stalin's dictatorship in Russia; they and their followers would most likely have been killed, and their movements would have died with them. In contrast, America's values of "In God We Trust," (there is an actual, higher Truth), "e pluribus unum" (from many, one), and "Liberty" have helped form a collective national character that encourages a respect for higher values, and the freedom of speech to try and sort through those values. Americans also tolerate disagreement from others as we debate these values. This competition of "may the best idea win" has been instrumental to the development of our superpower nation. See Dennis Prager's "Prager

University: The American Trinity" on YouTube for an informative elaboration of this critical point.

Our W.C.M.J. values are more than just a sword for our actions; they are also a shield of defense that helps protect our mental health. As Shannon French alluded to in her book, *Code of the Warrior*, a proper, value-based code of conduct may give soldiers or police the chance to sleep peacefully at night, even if they had to commit violence during the day. "Moral violence"—such as when a policeman must hit a man to stop him from raping a woman—although a lower level act, occasionally has a beneficial purpose.

At the same time, if people become corrupted with "errored morality," then a danger emerges that their misguided beliefs will lead them to perform horrible acts. When innocent civilians were killed during the September 11th attacks, or during the Mai Lai massacre of America's Vietnam operations, were the perpetrators acting as terrorists, soldiers, or martyrs for their cause? The perpetrators created terror, but they did not change the actions or values of the population that they were trying to influence. Their actions were brutal, but not effective in the long-term. An interesting reflection on the effects and limits of violence can be seen in the movie *Munich*.

Why Must We Persist?

There is one other value bias—persistence—that appears to be critical for our *Life* journey. Before we consider the science supporting this value, we should note that numerous achievers have also proclaimed the importance of persistence. Over 2,500 years ago in the East (China), Lao Tzu wrote in Chapter 33 of his book, *Tao Te Jing*, "He who acts with persistence has will."

2,500 years later, in the year 1909, Rudyard Kipling of the West (Britain) wrote his poem *If*:

If you can keep your head when all about you
Are losing theirs and blaming it on you,
If you can trust yourself when all men doubt you,
But make allowance for their doubting too;

If you can wait and not be tired by waiting,
Or being lied about, don't deal in lies,

Or being hated, don't give way to hating,
And yet don't look too good, nor talk too wise:

If you can dream - and not make dreams your master;
If you can think - and not make thoughts your aim;
If you can meet with Triumph and Disaster
And treat those two impostors just the same;

If you can bear to hear the truth you've spoken
Twisted by knaves to make a trap for fools,
Or watch the things you gave your life to broken,
And stoop and build 'em up with wornout tools:

If you can make one heap of all your winnings
And risk it on one turn of pitch-and-toss,
And lose, and start again at your beginnings
And never breathe a word about your loss;

If you can force your heart and nerve and sinew
To serve your turn long after they are gone,
And so hold on when there is nothing in you
Except the Will which says to them: 'Hold on!'

If you can talk with crowds and keep your virtue,
Or walk with kings - nor lose the common touch,
If neither foes nor loving friends can hurt you,
If all men count with you, but none too much;

If you can fill the unforgiving minute
With sixty seconds' worth of distance run -
Yours is the Earth and everything that's in it,
And - which is more - you'll be a Man my son!

Similarly, shortly after Rudyard's *If* was published, then-President
Calvin Coolidge offered his thoughts on persistence during a speech in the
year 1914:

"Nothing in the world can take the place of persistence.
Talent will not; nothing is more common

118

than unsuccessful men with talent.
Genius will not; unrewarded genius is almost a proverb.
Education will not; the world is full of educated derelicts.
Persistence and determination alone are omnipotent.
The slogan "Press on!" has solved and always will solve the problems of the human race."

All of these words of wisdom, across thousands of years, speak to the value of persistence. Scientific studies, such as those by Herbert Simon, have provided insights about why persistence is associated with achievement. Herbert analyzed experts of the game of chess. More specifically, he showed chess players (of varying skill levels) chess boards of partially played chess games. These boards had not been previously played by the players viewing the board. He then compared how the expert chess players differed from the beginning chess players in remembering the locations of the chess pieces. After numerous recall scenarios, Herbert concluded that the chess experts had a better recall of the pieces' locations. It was hypothesized that, since the experts had been exposed to so many scenarios during their numerous years of playing, they were able to reconstruct piece locations from "played games" with more ease than beginners.

To further test this hypothesis, he then placed chess pieces randomly on a board and asked all of the players to memorize the piece placements. Lacking any authentic game scenarios with which to compare random piece locations, the chess experts did not perform meaningfully better than the chess beginners. From experiments such as these, Herbert went on to propose a "10 Year rule" for developing expertise. Loosely paraphrased, it takes 10 years of experience to develop expertise in a skill. The real-world seems to support this "rule." For example, Tiger Woods did not just walk onto a golf course and win professional golf's premier tournament, *The Master's*. Tiger had already been playing at a championship level for over a decade (dating back to his multiple Junior World Golf and College Golf Championships).

A person such as Tiger Woods did not acquire expertise simply by practicing (shall we scrutinize his private life?). As Anders Ericsson has pointed out, expert practice involves "effortful study" or "deliberate practice." This type of practice is different from competition, primarily because during this "deliberate practice" a person deliberately works on the weaknesses in their overall game. This strategic use of time differs from a competition because people typically compete by playing to their strengths, and minimizing their use of weak techniques. Deliberately working on all aspects of a skill set—including your weaknesses—for the persistent length of at least 10 years—is associated with success.

Other researchers, such as Carol Dweck, have made similar conclusions about the value of persistence, but from a different perspective. She has reviewed numerous years of research on motivation. Her studies have led her to conclude that if parents want to raise smart children, then they should focus more on teaching their children to exert (persistent) effort, and less on acknowledging their child's intelligence. It is speculated that excessive praise might incline a child to take their abilities for granted and lead the child to subsequently not work as hard, or with as much persistence.

If we wish to build up our expertise in life, then we must integrate the value bias of persistence into our life. Earlier, in the *Money* Chapter, we discussed "core competencies"—the skills that you already do better than at least 80% of the rest of the population. Have you considered how you would like to develop those competencies? As the business man who was known as the "second richest man on the planet"—Andrew Carnegie—once said, "Put all of your eggs into one basket...and then watch that basket!" Perhaps our core competencies are the eggs within the basket of ourselves? Although the safest form of investing is to diversify your investments, many role modelers of expertise (e.g., athletes, business owners, etc.) demonstrate a strong case for investing heavily in one asset—yourself.

It may seem a little daunting, at first, to think that it might take 10 years to develop true expertise. However, compared to the alternative of developing no expertise, developing an expertise in something that you enjoy would appear to offer you more options for your future. I certainly have enjoyed the challenges and insights that this book journey has offered me during the last 10 years (researching useful information takes time!).

*****

To summarize the pursuit of expertise during your *Life* (e.g., the pursuit of a skill, or a value system, etc.), consider thinking of that choice using the principle of *opportunity cost*. You may choose the pain of growth, expertise, and achievement, and then enjoy the lasting satisfaction that accompanies it. Alternatively, you may choose the pain of regret that comes from growing nothing over time and then being haunted by a lasting hollowness as your grow older. Choose W.C.M.J.-ly...

Additional principles:

Value Biases (Utilitarian, Natural Law, Individual Liberty, Equality,
          Moral Relativism, Moral Absolutism)
Role Modeling
P.I.E.S.
W.C.M.J.
Persistence

For Further Reflection:

1) Who or what do you know that has shown to lead a happy, productive life? Can you explain the associated value systems?

2) What kind of values do you and your friends think are important to ask about partners?

      a. F.L.Y. – A.S.I.A.?
      b. P.I.E.S.?
      c. ScISSoRS?
      d. S.U.M.A. Love?
      e. What else?

3) How much do you and your current (or ideal) partner spend time asking questions about you, themselves, and your relationship? How many common values and goals unite you?

4) Do you trust your current partner? How long / what type of evidence did it take to achieve this level of trust?

5) On what issues are you and your partner like a Scientists (open), and on what issues are you and your partner like a Lawyer (defensive)?

6) Are you involved an argument? Is it because of a values conflict? What are the beginning biases of each side? Is it based upon earlier values from parents, friends, religion, or other influences?

7) If George Washington was a W.C.M.J. role model for leadership, do you or your friends have a W.C.M.J. role model for relationships? Money? Time?

8) Using deliberate practice, how might you overcome a weakness and build up strength in one of your relationship roles (e.g., "worker," "romantic partner," other)?

For Further Investigation:

John Darley and Daniel Batson, "From Jerusalem to Jericho": A study of Situational and Dispositional Variables in Helping Behavior." *Journal of Personality and Social Psychology*, 1973

Who Wants to Be a SuperHero, Season 1.

For a brief synopsis of the 2003 U of Mich Undergraduate Affirmative Action case, consider http://www.oyez.org/cases/2000-2009/2002/2002_02_516/ and http://www.oyez.org/cases/2000-2009/2002/2002_02_241/

Ward Connerly, *Creating Equal: My Fight Against Race Preferences*

Suzanne Sataline, "A Child's Death and a Crisis for Faith," Wall Street Journal, June 12 '08

For weight and obesity statistics, see: http://www.medicalnewstoday.com/articles/9542.php

Munich

More on Calvin Coolidge can be found at: http://www.conservativeforum.org/authquot.asp?ID=91

Lao Tsu, Jacob Needleman, Gia-Fu Feng, and Jane English, *Tao Te Ching*

Rudyard Kipling, *If*

Anders Ericsson, "The acquisition of expert performance: An introduction to some of the issues." in *The Road to Excellence: The Acquisition of Expert Performance in the Arts and Sciences, Sports, and Games*

Herbert Simon and William Chase, "Skill in chess." *American Scientist,* 1973

Carol Dweck, "The Secret to Raising Smart Kids," *Scientific American Mind*, Dec 2007

Decision-making: Getting to the POINT

"Chance favors only the prepared mind." — Louis Pasteur

Human versus computer—this intelligence contest achieved a historical first in 1997. Deep Blue, a chess-playing computer created by IBM, defeated reigning world chess champion Garry Kasparov by winning two games, losing one, and tying three during a 6-game match. With that victory, a question that had previously belonged to science fiction films (such as the *Terminator* series) became more real, "Would machines soon be more intelligent than humans?"

What is often forgotten about that "Kasparov vs. Deep Blue" matchup is that Garry Kasparov had previously defeated an earlier version of Deep Blue in 1996. In preparation for a rematch in 1997, IBM's design team increased the components and technologies associated with Deep Blue's evaluation functions. These upgrade processes included improving Deep Blue's "intelligence" by analyzing thousands of games from expert level chess players (presumably, this included reviewing games that Garry had played), as well as consulting with other chess grandmasters. At the same time, when Garry wanted to study the games that Deep Blue had played, IBM did not provide him with the Deep Blue histories. Which side do you think improved their chess-playing "intelligence" the most before the rematch?

Even during the rematch, Deep Blue's support team continued to improve Deep Blue's *ability to predict*. As Wikipedia has noted, the rules of the rematch allowed "...the developers to modify the [Deep Blue] program between games, an opportunity they said they used to shore up weaknesses in the computer's play revealed during the course of the match. This allowed the computer to avoid a trap in the final game that it had fallen for twice before."

Computer technology has continued to improve since Deep Blue's competitive days (Deep Blue was eventually dismantled), and most personal computers offer quite a challenge if you wish to play against them in games such as chess or Othello. Yet there is one game that continues to reveal the limits of "computer intelligence." The Chinese game of "Go," possibly the oldest human board game ever created, takes place on a board with a grid (usually formed with 19 x 19 intersecting lines). During the game, two players place their pieces on the board's grid in an attempt to control the majority of the board's surface. As simple as the game appears, the decision-making involved with Go overwhelms most computers' decision-making programs. Why?

Let us briefly contrast some of Go's features with chess's structure. Even though chess has different pieces with different capabilities, it only takes place on an 8 x 8 board, with an average of 20-40 moves possible during each turn. Given this relatively limited set of moves, a computer is often able to quickly evaluate all of the possible moves for that turn, as well as predict the next series of possible moves. After analyzing all of the options, the computer then chooses the most optimal move. This "brute force" prediction process works well within chess's "limited" possibilities. In contrast, the "brute force" process cannot optimize among all of the options within Go, because each turn offers a player an average of over 200 choices—too many "next moves!"

While Go highlights a limitation of computer decision-making, Go and other board games also highlight some of humankind's decision-making strengths. For example, skillful players can often determine if their opponents are making purposeful, strategic moves, or simply making nonsensical moves (once during a chess match with novice George Plimpton, Garry Kasparov was noted for looking at Plimpton's moves and remarking "What is this mess?"). Additionally, although there is uncertainty associated with an opponent's moves (the opponent could be bluffing), even relatively inexperienced players can interpret certain information about their opponents ("Is my opponent sweating?" "Nervous?"). Computers cannot yet perform this kind of "fuzzy logic" analysis.

Of course, neither computers nor humans can "brute force" predict the outcomes of more complex scenarios, such as *Life-altering* decisions, with one hundred percent accuracy (*Life* does not occur on a simple game grid).

125

Still, we may deliberately practice and improve our decision-making ability to a more skillful level. More specifically, we will use this chapter to think about thinking by focusing on the five stages of decision-making that allow us to "Get to the POINT":

P: **P**roblem determination.
O: **O**bjective of my response.
I: **I**f I choose this alternative…
N: **N**ow act!
T: **T**imely review and adjustment.

We will look at each of the five decision-making phases separately, and then combine them together to briefly look at a common graduate decision—job choice.

OF NOTE: If people perform the first POINT stage poorly, then no matter how well they perform the other four stages, they are more likely to make a poor decision. For this reason, we will spend a little extra time on the first stage of "Problem Determination." This will also allow us to uncover many of the common mistakes that people make when they start analyzing a problem, and improve our ability to achieve better outcomes.

P: Problem Determination

"What is the problem?"

Thousands of pages of research have been written about the flaws associated with how people determine a problem and its answer. For example, some people believe that they have the problem of "I do not have as much money as I would like." Is that really the problem? Using the technique of "The Three Wise Questions," people may better determine their actual problem. The "Wise" questions are "Why?", "Why?", and "Why?" For example, consider this young lady's problem:

"I do not have as much money as I would like."
    (Why?)
"…because I only work 20 hours per week…"
    (Why?)
"…because I go to school full-time (15 college credits)…"
    (Why?)

"...because I want to acquire an interesting job that pays a lot of money in the future..."

As a result of asking "Why?" three times, our student has gained a better understanding of her current problem. Perhaps a more precise definition of her problem would be "While I am in college full-time, I will not have as much money as I would like." In this case, the core problem appears to include a time control factor, and not just the money control factor that was initially stated. The Wise Questions technique, popularized by Sakichi Toyoda, has given our student a deeper understanding of her problem.

With this more-detailed "problem," she may consider the appropriate ways to resolve it. For example, if she is willing to accept the opportunity cost of "graduating later," then she might become a part-time student so that she may work more hours (it can be very challenging to work more than 20 hours per week while earning 15-18 college credits each term). Alternatively, she may prefer to finish college—and earn higher pay— sooner, and become more comfortable with the fact that her "money during school" situation is only a temporary condition.

As a contrast, consider this young gentleman's Three Wise Questions to the same problem:

"I do not have as much money as I would like."
    (Why?)
"...because I am in a low-paying, 40-hour-a-week job..."
    (Why?)
"...because I do not have any skills that are worth higher wages..."
    (Why?)
"...because I have not started any skills training programs..."

This young man's more precise problem might be better stated as "I do not have the skills necessary to earn the amount of money that I would like." This suggests that he should focus on acquiring some valued skills. Whether by learning through a community college vocational program, apprenticing with a craftsman (such as a brick layer), or training in some other skills arena, he has found a credible answer to his more precise problem by using the Three Wise Questions.

As a final example, let us consider how The Three Wise Questions might need to become The *Five* Wise Questions or even The *Seven* Wise Questions as a person tries to determine their real problem (versus their surface problem). For example, consider this young lady's problem:

"I do not have the kind of romantic life that I would like."
(Why?)
"…because I am lonely…"
(Why?)
"…because no one talks to me unless they have to (usually at work)…"

(Why?…and notice how two different responses occur…more are possible…let us look at each separately)
…the first response:

"…because I have not joined interactive groups."
(Why?)
"…because I have not looked for an interesting group."
(Why?)
"…because I have been busy."

…a possible second response:

"…I do not start any conversations."
(Why?)
"…I am shy."
(Why?)
"…I have nothing to talk about."

…we will stop this scenario at the *Five* Question level (two Whys plus alternative sets of three Whys). Can you see how she has moved away from the initial "problem?" During her responses, our graduate has revealed that she has been prioritizing other activities at the opportunity cost of "participating in group activities." She has also felt that she does not have much to talk about. By participating in group activities, even if she is only able to say the word "Hi" at first, she will build up relationships through common experiences that everyone may discuss. Coincidentally, she will also expand her network of people connections, which may also increase her chance of meeting a future romantic partner—at least these group activities increase her chances more than if she stayed at home and watched television.

Although the Three Wise Questions (or Five, or Seven) help us to better determine our problem, there can be additional biases that cloud our ability to understand the challenges that we encounter. These biases influence our interpretation of the world, just as they did during the *Values* chapter scenario "Choose between three lives or one within a burning building." As you start to determine your problems, you will want to account for at least four biases:

1.   Self-interest
2.   Group
3.   Historical
4.   Magnitude

The first bias involves self-interest—what is the main interest of the individual who is involved in the situation?

Let us return to our earlier gentleman's problem of "I do not have as much money as I would like." This time, the core problem (after a few rounds of "Why?") is "I spend more money than I earn." Suppose that he wants to "solve" his problem by being paid more for the work that he does for his organization. His manager might not be able to give him that raise because the manager might have the problem "I cannot pay my people as much as I would like" (perhaps less money is available because the cost of the pensions for the company's workers has continued to rise). Under these circumstances, if the young man visits his boss and says, "I would like a raise in my earnings," then a conflict of self-interests might emerge between them.

Conflicts of bias can also occur within people because of group prejudices. For example, how would you respond to the problem "Our company does not have enough good people working here." If you choose a solution "Hire more good people," would you be biased in the way that you hired your next set of workers? The research conducted by Marianne Bertrand and Sendhil Mullainathan suggests that some people would be biased. Marianne and Sendhil created a series of fake resumes with identical credentials, but different names—names that would commonly be associated with Black people and White people. They then sent out the applications and resumes to over 1,000 employers. When they analyzed the responses, Marianne and Sendhil discovered that the applications and resumes with White-sounding names were 50 percent more likely to be contacted for a job interview than those applications that contained Black-sounding names.

Apparently, group prejudices can be a part of some people's biases when they review applications.

Unfortunately, biases can also extend to "in person" applications, as a study by Claudia Goldin and Cecilia Rouse demonstrated. Claudia and Cecilia noted that during the 1970s, women made up less than five percent of the musicians in the top five U.S. symphony orchestras. Women's presence eventually grew to 25 percent by the 1990s. Why? What was the difference? Claudia and Cecilia pointed out that during the later 1970s and the 1980s, orchestras began using "blind auditions" by having the applicants perform behind a screen. This type of blinding process kept the gender of the applicant secret—only the applicant's music could be heard. Under "blind" circumstances, more women were hired. Claudia and Cecilia found that the switch to using blind auditions seemed to account for (roughly) 30 to 50 percent of the increase in the hiring of female musicians.

Besides the more visible biases of group prejudice and self-interest, a third, less obvious bias occurs because of history. For example, suppose that a group of assembly line workers has been paid $55 per hour for their work. If they are suddenly told that they will only be paid $35 per hour to do the same job, then they would probably feel as though the $35 wage represented a loss of $20 per hour. At the same time, consider a town where no assembly manufacturing has been occurring, and the best job in town has been paying $25 per hour. If a new assembly plant is built in that town, and the people are offered $35 per hour to work at that factory, then the new wages look like a great improvement of $10 per hour. The same wage can represent a loss or a gain depending on how prior experiences have biased people's evaluations of the event.

This kind of historical bias occasionally occurs in relationships. We shall loosely label this bias *The Schmuck Effect*. The Schmuck Effect occurs when a previous bad relationship, or string of bad relationships, creates an impression in a graduate's mind that other people only act as self-interested users, and not as growth-oriented partners. If a graduate eventually develops low expectations of partner compatibility, then dating a merely "average" compatible person will seem like a large improvement. The resulting relationship might even be the best relationship that either person has ever known. However, this new relationship could be like going from a brutal job that pays $2 per hour to a less brutal job that pays $10 per hour—even though an interesting job that pays $20 per hour exists, since it has not been discovered, the $10 per hour job looks great. Similarly, some people settle for an "average relationship" because the risks and uncertainty of finding a really good partner seems like too much work (or too unlikely). They stop at some "acceptable" level of compatibility.

Yet skillful onlookers, who are in growth-oriented relationships, might still look at these "acceptable" relationship partners and ask, "What are those two doing together?" The onlookers would know that time spent in an "average" relationship comes with an opportunity cost—the chance to look for, and possibly someday join, a better-matching partner (perhaps a "$35 per hour" relationship is out there...$50?). "Settling" for a mediocre relationship is often labeled as "rebound" behavior, and this biased decision typically occurs after a romantic relationship breaks up.

To combat this type of historical bias, we need to identify what we want from our partnerships. The problem of "I do not have a romantic partner" is much easier to solve than "I do not have a compatible, growth-oriented relationship." Additionally, we must avoid creating problem determinations such as "I want someone who is better than my last partner"—if the last partner was "extremely low compatibility," then "low compatibility" will seem like an improvement.

Instead, graduates should develop expectations, such as the ScISSoRS standards, so that they may evaluate their relationship options against objective standards, and not historical biases. Patience may be necessary, because if people do not want another *Schmuck* for a date, then they must be prepared to remain single if they do not immediately encounter a good-matching partner. As always, the R of ScISSoRS applies—Reciprocity—people must be willing to give as much to their partner as they are expecting to receive.

It is interesting how dating options have evolved to more rapidly reveal whether or not someone will meet another person's standards. In the old days, you might hope to learn about a potential partner from friends or group activities. Now, activities such as speed-dating offer you the chance to state what you desire up front (sometimes in 5 minutes or less). Similarly, websites such as www.eHarmony.com use a series of questions to uncover deeper personal compatibility information about potential partners, without requiring participants to "invest" in a first date (or second? or third?). Perhaps future research will examine whether these techniques improved people's odds of predicting a good-matching, long-term partner.

One other historical bias is known as the "sunk cost" bias. As an example of this bias, suppose that a group of students go to a movie theater and each member pays $8 to watch a movie. After the first 15 minutes of watching the movie, they all conclude that they do not like it. If there is a "no refund" policy at that movie theater, some of the students will say "Well, I paid for this garbage, I might as well watch it" and stay for the entire show. Understandably, people do not enjoy throwing money away. However, notice that the $8 is already a "sunk cost"—the money has been spent and it cannot be returned—it is "sunk." Looking forward in time, the only relevant question for each student is "Which opportunity, as well as opportunity costs, should I pursue during the next hour and a half—should I stay at this movie, or should I go do something else?" If remaining at the movie mentally drains the students, then perhaps they should use that personal time for something else, such as a nap.

Of course, the more we commit to a situation (e.g., a project, a career, a relationship), the harder it can become to objectively examine its costs and benefits. It also becomes more difficult to walk away from your "heavy investment" situations, even when they are bad situations. For example, have you ever encountered a person who seems rather uninspired by their current partner? When you ask them why they continue to stay together with their significant other, the only justification they can come up with is "because I have invested so much of myself in this relationship." There is no mention of future growth goals, only the sunk costs of the past.

Apparently, some couples prefer to stay in their somewhat mediocre (or less) relationship rather than risk the uncertainties associated with living single and possibly seeking a better-matching partner. Yet a bad relationship is a bad relationship, even if someone has already "invested" two years in it. People can combat this relationship "sunk cost bias" by beginning their relationship analysis with a statement such as, "No matter what has happened in my past, from this moment forward, the relevant relationship opportunities and costs in my life are…"

One additional historical bias that sometimes appears in romantic and work relationships occurs when you examine a routine and ask "Why do we do it this way?" If you ask that question at work, your boss may answer with the historical justification of "because that is the way we have always done it." You might choose to counter this "argument" by stating that "Times have changed" and then list what makes the current situation different. Otherwise, such historical behavior will continue. As an example, consider summer school breaks. They were originally designed so that the children of farming families could help harvest the fields. Today, only a small percentage of America's population actually farm for a living, yet the summer vacations remain in many school systems. Some people believe that the extra personal time of summer offers children more opportunities to be mischievous, while others propose that the unstructured space has allowed American children to develop more creativity. Either way, summer breaks exist even though the original purpose of the break rarely applies, and few people have questioned the continuation of it.

The final bias that we will consider is how the "magnitude" of an event influences us. For example, people's perspective of cost becomes blurred when they purchase expensive goods such as a new car or house. With "thousands of dollars" becoming the reference value that people use, many people cannot accurately gage the impact of purchasing extra design options and upgrades. For example, a person who would not ordinarily pay $600 for a car stereo does not react as negatively to that price when it is bundled within a $20,000 automobile price. Combat this type of magnitude bias by comparing products against your needs, versus your wants. This technique will give you a more objective standard when you go shopping.

Another interesting distortion of magnitude can occur when people receive money that they did not earn. Whether by the luck of a lottery, birthday card generosity from a grandparent, or some other good fortune, some people spend "bonus" money more easily than if they had been forced to earn that same amount. One dollar still equals a dollar—regardless of the source. However, since gift money recipients did not have to shift any of their priorities, relationships, or time to acquire the funds, some find it easier to spend the money. Combat this "bonus" money bias by asking yourself, "how long would I have to work in order to save this much?" (whether by working extra hours, coupon clipping, etc.). Referencing your budget to see how much "uncommitted money" you have at the end of each pay period will help reveal just how long it would take for you gain an amount of "earned money" equal to the unearned "bonus money."

One last magnitude bias that we should examine is the bias that comes from using percentages. For example, in the year 2007 there were headlines that declared "Kidney failure increasing in cats by 30%." "30%" certainly sounds like a large magnitude. However, if you were to read deeper into the facts, you would have learned that the original kidney failure rate was around "2.3 cats per 10,000." The 30% increase meant that "3 cats per 10,000" were now experiencing kidney failure. While the increase in kidney failures was certainly a sad event for some cat owners, it is curious that the news sources chose to emphasize the kidney failure increase by referring to the "large" percent change, instead of the "less than 1 per 10,000" raw number change. To avoid being overwhelmed by a large statistic, check both the raw number change and the percent change.

So far, we have been focusing on the major biases within our Problem Determination step (P OINT). This intelligence training was necessary because the better we can sort through the biases affecting our understanding of an event, the easier it will be to use our intelligence—the ability to accurately predict—to form the objective of our response. For more insight into biases and the decision-making process, consider reading Malcolm Gladwell's *Blink,* John Nofsinger's *Psychology of Investing,* and Barry Schwartz's *The Paradox of Choice.* As always, these are just some of my preferences. Perhaps when you look them up on the internet, or look across the shelves of a bookstore, you will find a better match for your current interests.

O: Objective of My Response

The objective of your response should be linked to the problem that you previously determined. To demonstrate how the Problem and Objective portion of PO INT decision-making relate, let us consider an example. Suppose that you determined that you have the problem of "I am not as fit as I would like to be." After reading a few articles on exercise and nutrition, as well as seeking advice from people that you consider to be reasonably healthy and fit, you determine that your objective for the next few months could be summarized by the following mantra: "Move a little more, eat a little less."

Later, when you turn on the television, by amazing coincidence, you see an info-mercial for a new piece of exercise equipment—the Wonder Machine. The announcer claims that "The Wonder Machine will make you more fit!" But will it? Will buying the Wonder Machine and using it be the right response to your problem?

Evaluating the claim that the Wonder Machine will make you more fit requires using a Scientist's mind. Proving that "Factor A (using the Wonder Machine) causes Result B (I am more fit)" requires that three conditions be satisfied:

#1. "A" must occur before "B."
#2. Changes in "B" are associated with increases or decreases in "A."
#3. No other simultaneous explanation for the changes in "B" exists.

Condition #1 (A must occur before B) provides an initial analysis of the situation. As you watch the info-mercial, you see super-buff studs and babes flexing their muscles as they exercise on the Wonder Machine. The advertisement seems to imply that the machine will <u>cause</u> you, a potential buyer, to become super-buff as well. Yet you consider the time question raised by Condition #1—did these super-buff people use the Wonder Machine before they became so buff? If the Wonder Machine has just been created, and these studs and babes are already super-buff, then it seems likely that these super-buff users were already in shape before the machine was built. Since the info-mercial did not provide proof of causal condition #1, you decide to not buy the Wonder Machine. You will take up walking instead.

Later that evening, another strange coincidence occurs. While listening to the radio, you happen to win a contest where the prize is a Wonder Machine. You pick up your Wonder Machine the next day, and the radio station takes your picture. You go home, read the directions, and decide to conduct your own "causality" experiment that will test whether using the Wonder Machine is associated with a change in your fitness level (condition #2). You begin your experiment by using the Wonder Machine for two hours per week during the first month. After that month (and some initial soreness), you decide to increase your Wonder Machine exercise time to four hours per week. Four weeks later, you notice that you are definitely more toned than you were the month before—increasing the Factor A of Wonder Machine exercise has resulted in a change—in this case an increase—in the factor B of fitness. Perhaps a claim can now be made that the Wonder Machine has affected your shape?

Almost unbelievably, one more coincidence occurs. You check your mail and see a postcard from The Wonder Machine Corporation. They are inviting you to make a statement about your how your body—and life—has changed as a result of the Wonder Machine. In fact, they would like your healthy-looking (even if not super-buff) person to appear on a commercial and state the following, "Now that I work out on the Wonder Machine, I have tight abs and a toned body." You stop to consider whether you can credibly make such a claim.

You consider the condition #3 for causality—no other explanation for the change in "B" (becoming more fit) exists. Certainly, you can claim that the Wonder Machine provided you with a focus for your motivated efforts to become more fit. You definitely move around more and burn more calories. So you feel that the Wonder Machine should be given some credit.

At the same time, you are hesitant to give the Wonder Machine full credit. This is a wise hesitation. Whenever we hear a claim that some factor

135

has caused human behavior to change, we must remember that there are at least two individual factors that "simultaneously compete" for a causal claim—*an individual's ability* and *an individual's level of effort.* For example, you may have previously played on a sports team in high school, or taken a weight training class. Given that experience, you have a greater *ability* to use the Wonder Machine than someone who has never used exercise equipment. "On average," you will be more capable of trying different exercises on the Wonder Machine, as well as developing comfortable, results-producing routines.

Your individual level of *effort* also affects the Wonder Machine's impact on your fitness level. A number of people order exercise equipment, get bored with it, and forget about exercising until the next interesting info-mercial comes along (notice how you do not see these bored people's testimonials on any info-mercial?). You, on the other hand, have the ability to focus your efforts (after all, you are already reading Chapter 6 of 8). You chose to try the Wonder Machine, and if it had not helped you achieve your fitness goals, then you would have returned it within 90 days, claimed your money-back guarantee, and then used that money to try something else until you achieved your desired outcomes (perhaps you would have tried walking non-stop for an hour at a time, four times per week).

Additionally, because you chose to use the Wonder Machine, you experienced an opportunity cost of NOT being able to sit in front of a television and snack for an additional four hours each week. In fact, as part of your overall fitness plan, you also ate a little less junk food, drank a little more water, and slept a little more. These lifestyle improvements increased your ability to digest food more rapidly and acquire a flatter stomach faster.

So with a clean conscience you go to the Wonder Machine studios and state the claim that, "The Wonder Machine has definitely helped me to become more fit." You also show "before" and "after" pictures of yourself, implying that the Wonder Machine was a key factor in your body's change. At the same time, you avoid making a fuller causal claim such as "I eat and drink the same items, view the same amount of TV, and get the same amount of sleep. The only thing different about me is that I added 4 hours of the Wonder Machine exercises to my weekly activities. Only the Wonder Machine has caused me to become more fit." Such a claim would be implausible. By adding in four hours of Wonder Machine activity, you necessarily reduced four hours of doing something(s) else.

(OF NOTE: When watching exercise or diet pill commercials, look for the written or fast-spoken verbal disclaimers such as "results not typical" or "this product, when combined with moderate exercise and a healthy diet, produces results." Is it really the pill or the new exercise machine that caused the change? If people always moderately exercised and ate reasonably healthy diets, would any new exercise product actually "cause" better fitness?)

In support of the imaginary Wonder Machine example, real evidence from research suggests that "moving more" will lead to a better fitness outcome. For example, it has often been wondered why the Europeans seem to be thinner than Americans. David Bassett and his colleagues believe that they have a reasonable answer—the Europeans are much more likely to travel to work by walking, riding a bike, or using mass transit systems and then walking the final distance to work. With their greater likelihood of active movement as a standard part of their day, Europeans are also more likely to have lower obesity rates in their population (around 10 – 15%) compared to the United States "commuter" population (approximately 25-30%). While David and his colleagues do not make a causal claim, they seem to have uncovered evidence that, at a minimum, closely fulfills the first two conditions of causality and suggests that more movement lowers your chances of becoming obese. For an interesting approach to health and fitness, consider reading John Douillard's book *Mind, Body, and Sport*. For other explorations of interesting causal claims, consider reading *Freakonomics*, by Steven Levitt and Stephen Dubner.

I: If I choose this alternative...

After you have determined your problem and developed an objective for your response, there may be a number of ways to achieve that objective (PO I NT). For example, if you were seeking to become more fit, you might choose to walk or bike to work instead of drive. Given a choice among various alternatives, you may have to prioritize which alternative you want to try first. To help guide you on your journey of prioritization, you will most likely need to consider two major factors—the amount of uncertainty and the degree of satisfaction that you would like associated with your efforts.

Let us begin with uncertainty, and its close analytic partner "risk." Suppose that someone offers you one of two gifts. The first gift is $100. The second gift is a bit more complex, and it involves a quarter. It is a typical quarter, with typical weight. It is not a trick quarter. If someone were to flip that coin, we would expect that it would land on "heads" 50 percent of the time and "tails" the other 50 percent. Now, imagine that someone offered you a choice of either $100, or two hundred flips of a coin and the promise that you would receive a dollar every time the result was "heads." After thinking about it, you calculate that "coin flip gift" is, statistically speaking, worth $100 (200 flips x an expected 50% heads = 100 heads = $100). So, statistically speaking, "on average" you should be neutral between the two "gifts."

But are you? Do you feel that the "coin flip gift" is really worth $100? In theory, there could be 200 flips in a row where the result is "tails" and you receive $0. Alternatively, there could also be 200 "heads" in a row, and you could end up with $200. If you think that, on average, the guaranteed $100 and the "coin flip gift" are the same, then your level of risk-taking is typically labeled as "risk neutral." However, if you feel that the uncertainty of the outcome from the coin flips makes the "coin flip gift" worth less than $100, then you are known as "risk averse." Finally, if you believe that the "coin flip gift" is worth more than $100, you are likely a "risk seeker" who believes that you can beat the odds.

Asked another way, "What is the appropriate price of the 'coin flip gift?'" Would you rather have the certainty of $80, or the uncertain potential of the "200 flips?" What about the certainty of $30 versus the "coin flip gift?" What would make you absolutely indifferent between the "coin flip gift" with all of its uncertainty, and a sure thing of $____ (fill in your amount)? How does your answer compare with your friends and family? Would your comfort level with uncertainty change if the issue was no longer a hypothetical $100, but was instead your own long-term monetary investments and relationship choices?

An interesting thought experiment involving uncertainty and probability can be developed from the works of Blaise Pascal and Rene Descartes. Blaise suggested that if we were going to make a wager about whether or not there was a God, and live accordingly, then we should consider the outcomes from our choices. Instead of "heads" and "tails," we now must choose between "I believe that there is a God" and "I do not believe that there is a God."

If we choose "I believe that there is a God" and we live a God-centered value code, and we are right, then when we die we shall likely receive (according to most religions) an infinitely great reward. If we are wrong, then when we die we shall receive nothing.

Alternatively, if we choose "I do not believe that there is a God," and act accordingly, then if we are right, when we die we shall receive nothing. However, if we are wrong, and God does exist, then when we die it is possible that we will receive nothing, or something painfully worse, for our non-belief.

Both approaches offer a "nothing" option, but only one offers "great reward," while the other offers "great pain." On the basis of these outcomes—great reward or nothing if "belief," nothing or great pain if "non-belief"—it seems wiser to follow the "If" of "I believe that there is a God" and live accordingly.

Additionally, even if there is only a slight chance, perhaps 0.00000000001% chance of there being a God, then mathematically:

0.00000000001% x infinite reward = infinite reward
(recall that, in math, anything x infinity = infinity)

So, is there a slight chance that God exists? Rene Descartes provided an interesting ontological argument that makes the 0.00000000001% seem likely. Paraphrasing some of the Rene's broader points, a person might reflect on the following thoughtful steps:

1. Can I conceive of "perfection?"
2. Yes, although it is not often a human trait, I can conceive of "perfection."
3. I think I shall call that perfection "God."
4. Now, would that perfect God be good or evil?
5. A perfect God would be good.
6. Would that perfectly good God exist, or would that perfectly good God be absent from the universe and neglect it?
7. A perfectly good God would exist.

… given this thought process, the chance of God's existence seems likely, or at least better than 0.00000000001%. Play around with the logic and see what you conclude…as a deeper thought exercise, consider how this logic compares with the proofs of other "unseen" forms, such as Black Holes.

On to something slightly more "earthy"…as we decide among alternatives, we might wish to consider what degree of satisfaction we want from our desired outcomes. A few examples will help clarify this concept.

Suppose that you need to buy a pencil. You enter a store and go straight to the aisle with office supplies. To your surprise, there are over 25 varieties of pencil to choose from, ranging from the standard #2 wooden pencil, to a variety of lead pencils with cushion grip handles. If you were going to find the optimal pencil, then you might interact with each pencil product for two minutes apiece as you make imaginary air writing gestures and consider each pencil's comfort. With two minutes of review for each product, you would invest 50 minutes in the process. If you then compared the top five pencils of the aisle, you might require another 10 minutes.

You could easily spend an hour looking for an *optimal* pencil, or you could just grab a pencil that writes, pay for it, and exit the store. The risk involved with a pencil purchase is usually low—$2.00 or less. Given that low level of money involved, you could even buy a second, different pencil type, just in case you really do not like the first pencil's performance. Then again, you may not feel that doing the pencil research to an optimal level merits your important time. Your degree of satisfaction might simply be "I want a pencil that writes" and not "I want a pencil that is so light and easy to write with that I can barely tell when it is resting in my hand." Your "good enough" attitude may not necessarily result in the optimal solution. At the same time, the additional costs from seeking greater pencil satisfaction may not be worth the minimal extra benefit. You might be comfortable with "settling."

When it comes to bigger decisions, such as romance (you cannot buy two spouses), or making a large purchase (you cannot, usually, afford to buy two cars at one time), the costs of seeking optimal (or nearly optimal) satisfaction might be worth your time. Focusing on optimal conditions will allow you to choose what you value most. For example, suppose that you were wanting to buy a new car, and the four ideal characteristics of that car would be that it looks cool, accelerates quickly, achieves great gas mileage, and is relatively inexpensive. After shopping around for a while, you eventually narrow down your decision to a choice between two different vehicles. The first vehicle—the Dragon—looks cooler and accelerates faster than the second vehicle, the Mule. Yet the Mule has its merits. It costs less and achieves better gas mileage than the Dragon. How will you decide between the two "if" options?

	Mule	Dragon
Gas mileage	35 mpg	25 mpg
Price	$19,500	$23,000
Acceleration	0 – 60 in 6.2 seconds	0 – 60 in 5 seconds
Looks	non-distinct	Stylishly Intense

If all four factors mattered equally in your decision, then you would have a hard time choosing between the two vehicles because each car has two of the factors that you value most. However, after you consider what you actually need the car for—transportation to and from work (a 10 mile, mostly city, drive), you decide to prioritize your four characteristics as follows: Gas mileage, Price, Acceleration, Looks.

Now the decision of "If I choose this car" becomes much clearer. The Mule, while not as quick or visually attractive as the Dragon, represents the better vehicle (according to your values) because it meets your highest priorities.

However, the very next day an unexpected event occurs—a local car dealer who bought too many Dragons for his sales lot is now offering Dragons for $4,000 less than the listed price. Now, the Dragon at $19,000 is the better match for three of your vehicle priorities. Is that enough to overcome the Mule's advantage of gas mileage, your number one priority?

To answer this question, you decide to go one step further with your priority list—you add a "favoritism weight" to each of your priorities. To do that, you pick a number ("100" in this case) and distribute the 100 points among the priorities. For example, if all four car factors mattered equally, then you would write the priorities as:

Favoritism Weight	
Gas mileage	25
Price	25
Acceleration	25
Looks	25

However, all four characteristics do not matter equally. For the purpose of this example, you decide that gas mileage is where half of your decision-making should come from (50 points), while price is also significantly important (30 points). At the same time, acceleration and looks are really not that important for your "commute to work" vehicle, so you allocate the remaining points to these factors with the values of 12 and 8, respectively. Now your prioritized choices look like:

	Favoritism Weight
Gas mileage	50
Price	30
Acceleration	12
Looks	8

... to further focus your preference, you decide to include how well the Mule and the Dragon match each of your priorities (a scale of 1-10 usually works, with "10" being an optimal match). For example, suppose that you thought 40 miles per gallon would be a "Perfect 10" for meeting your expectations. In that case, you could look at the Mule's gas mileage of 35 m.p.g. and calculate that the Mule has earned an 8.8 on a 10 point scale for gas mileage (35/40 = .875), while the Dragon has earned a score of 6.3 out of 10 (25/40 = .625). You place those scores along the row of the Gas mileage priority with the Favoritism Weight of 50.

	Favoritism Weight	Mule-Perfect 10 match?	Dragon?
Gas mileage	50	8.8	6.3

You then move on to the next priority—price. Suppose that an amazing price of $16,000 would have been a "Perfect 10" out of 10 for meeting this priority. You might then choose to value that every $1,000 more than $16,000 is worth 1 point less on the Perfect 10 scale. So, the Mule earns a score of 6.5 ($19,500 - $16,000 = $3,500, or 3.5 points deducted from a Perfect 10), while the Dragon earns a score of 7 ($19,000 - $16,000 = $3,000, or 3.0 points deducted from a Perfect 10). You also develop what seems like reasonable scores for acceleration (the Dragon was nearly "hyper quick" when you test drove it. The Mule? Not so much...). Lastly, the Mule had acceptable, "non-distinct" looks, while the Dragon was "stylishly intense." You complete your analysis chart and it looks like the following:

	Favoritism Weight	Mule-Perfect 10 match?	Dragon?
Gas mileage	50	8.8	6.3
Price	30	6.5	7.0
Acceleration	12	6.0	9.5
Looks	8	6.0	9.5

One final step remains: multiply the "Perfect 10" columns for each vehicle by the "Favoritism Weight" that you assigned to each category. For example, the final value of gas mileage for the Mule is 440 because a "Favoritism Weight" of 50, times an 8.8 "Perfect 10" score, equals 440. The rest of the results follow:

	Favoritism Weight		Mule-Perfect 10 match?	Dragon?
Gas mileage	50	x	8.8 = 440	6.3 = 315
Price	30	x	6.5 = 195	7.0 = 210
Acceleration	12	x	6.0 = 72	9.5 = 114
Looks	8	x	6.0 = 48	9.5 = 76
Total worth according to your Values:			755	715

Given your values, which in this case greatly favored gas mileage, the Mule is still the better buy for you, even though the Dragon was preferred on three out of the four factors. However, if you were really interested in buying a great looking vehicle (perhaps to represent your new status as a graduate), then if you re-valued the "gas mileage" and "looks" Favoritism Weights to each be worth 29, the Dragon vehicle would now be your car of choice (by a score of 782 to 696...see for yourself!).

Your favoritism and "meet a Perfect 10" weights will likely differ from mine—personal preferences vary. The more important lesson from this somewhat lengthy exercise is that this type of multi-characteristic decision-making (MCDM) that we just performed can help you intelligently decide which big investments, within an "if" list of choices, will be most satisfying.

We have now practiced defining our problem, proposing an objective that would solve our problem, and comparing our "if" alternatives with regards to risks and levels of satisfaction. It is time for the next step of...

N: Now act!

You are now (POI N T) ready for action. As a final focus of the "If" action that you have chosen, consider using the technique inspired by Peter Drucker's work *The Practice of Management*—use "S.M.A.R.T." actions. More specifically, deliberately practice your efforts to be:

S: **S** pecific
M: **M** easurable
A: **A** ttainable
R: **R** esults-oriented
T: **T** ime-dated

For example, an effort should <u>not</u> be "to become fit"—that is too vague. To be S.M.A.R.T. about how you reach your fitness destination, you might phrase your action as "I will either walk, or use the Wonder Machine, for one hour per day, 4 days per week, for the next 4 weeks." This type of S.M.A.R.T. statement focuses you. It **s**pecifically states what you will do in a **m**easurable way (4 hours). It keeps you grounded in an **a**ttainable reality— four hours per week is a reasonable allocation of time. The S.M.A.R.T. statement is designed to achieve **r**esults (e.g., more exercise, more fitness), and it contains a **t**ime period for accomplishing your actions. Other S.M.A.R.T. statements you might consider include "I will drink 32 ounces of water each day for this entire week." or "I will consume only one serving of a dessert each day."

Some people create variations on the S.M.A.R.T. model. They may say "I will only consume 1,600 calories each day until I reach the weight suggested by my doctor." For this type of goal, the time period does not have a specific number of days, which helps reduce the intensity of the goal, compared to a goal such as "I will lose 5 pounds in 5 days"—probably not a healthy goal. As always, it is recommended that you consult a physician or other qualified exercise expert before beginning a fitness routine.

T: Timely Review and Adjustment

After you have begun your S.M.A.R.T. action, you will want to allocate time to review it and see if you are achieving the causal results that you were expecting (POIN $\boxed{\text{T}}$). For example, if you exercise with the Wonder Machine and are able to do more repetitions or heavier exertions with greater ease, then your exercise actions may indeed be <u>causing</u> you to become stronger and more fit.

You might also use your review time to consider how unexpected factors may have affected your actions and outcomes. For example, if you became sick, it would be unrealistic, or at least not very practical, to believe that you would have continued to exercise at your typical intensity level during your illness week (or weeks). The illness may have delayed your progress toward your future goal(s), and you may have to reset your time table—it might now take you five weeks to accomplish what you had previously planned would take you four. That is quite acceptable. Be willing to adjust your expectations if an unexpected external event interferes with your actions and outcomes. For more insight into the impact of the unexpected, consider reading Nassim Taleb's *The Black Swan*.

The P.O.I.N.T. of Your Work Choices

Now that you have seen each of the pieces of the P.O.I.N.T. system, let us consider how the whole system might help guide your decisions about your jobs choices. Most of us spend a large part of our adult waking hours at, going to, or returning from, work. Compared to buying a pencil, choosing a job appears to be a decision worth the extra effort of a full P.O.I.N.T. analysis.

As we now know, the first phase of our decision process is the "Problem determination." A possible "problem" that ultimately leads us to work could be "My parents are not going to pay for my upkeep beyond age 18 (or perhaps 22 in the case of some college students)." Most of us have not won a lottery, inherited a fortune, or worked enough in high school to retire from active work. Therefore, we must develop a work objective as our response. This can be tougher than it sounds.

For example, some people prefer to work in a "drone" job. Drones, like the bees in a hive, perform jobs that are comprised of repetitive tasks. This type of work, while not always exciting, answers the money demands of many workers. Workers may find satisfaction in their routine work, and may not want to risk changing to a new job environment. For some, their job objective is "safe, steady pay."

(Of course, America is no longer the sole business power on the planet, so no job should be regarded as completely safe and secure. We must be cautious about ever believing that employment is guaranteed or an entitlement.)

Other graduates may have a job objective of "earn as much money as possible in my 20s." They perceive their job (or jobs) as a tool that they will use to build up extra money so that they can later pursue the goals that they desire. They are internally driven to save for great adventures like buying a dream home, traveling to foreign lands, or helping create shelters for the

145

homeless. Some of these people will also pack their own lunches, move closer to work, and work 70 hours per week to earn double-time pay (or work a second job) for years. These graduates sacrifice part of their "now" for the future, making the struggle endurable because they live in alignment with their ultimate goals.

Still others will want to select a job that they really enjoy, and then adjust their spending habits accordingly. By having a job that they enjoy so much that they would almost be willing to do it for free, their work does not feel burdensome. It is a pleasure. If people can keep their spending habits balanced with the pay of their favorite job, then they will feel less stress from two of life's most pressing challenges—finding meaningful work while being content with the pay that it offers. They have the job objective "I want to do something interesting, and get paid for doing it."

Whatever your work objective, you will no doubt need to consider (or have already considered) the "If" choice of whether to pursue additional schooling to help you reach your job goal(s). These "If" choices, as we discussed in the *Money* chapter, come with opportunity costs. Still, a college degree, or a two-year technical degree, typically represents to employers that an applicant can independently manage complexity. Some companies do not actually need their employees to possess a college degree, but they use the degree as a type of signal of *effort* and *ability*. For employers, those applicants who have earned a degree, or a professional certificate (i.e., software, CPA, therapist) have shown an ability to independently motivate themselves and responsibly prioritize an opportunity.

A subtle distinction about an applicant's potential, as signaled by their education, seems appropriate at this point. It is fairly well accepted that the more education you obtain, the higher your earnings will be. "On average," this appears to be true. However, after a certain level of education, that causal relationship breaks down. For example, a person with a Master's degree in Business Administration (M.B.A.) will probably start out earning more than a person with a Ph.D. in Medieval French History.

For the purposes of a PO I NT demonstration, let us assume that you believed that an MBA was the best path for your future job choices, and that you are just about to graduate from an MBA program that is ranked in the "Top 30." You are at the "If" phase of choosing between two job offers—a $115,000 per year job located in Big City, USA, and a $75,000 per year job located in Medium City. Both jobs appear to have similar responsibilities. How might you begin to choose between them?

146

First, to help you combat the magnitude bias, you might use a "cost of living" website, such as the www.CNNmoney.com website listed at the end of this chapter, to compare how expensive it is to live in Big City, versus Medium City. After considering the cost difference, you might also investigate the time difference associated with the two jobs. Commute time is an opportunity cost that too many people overlook. Some people will drive an hour, one-way, or take a commuter rail to get to work in Big City so that they may live in a nice area away from work. However, if you live are able to live in a nice area that is only 15 minutes away from work in Medium City, then compared to the Big City employees who commute one hour each way, you would gain an extra hour and a half of personal time each day. That is like being handed extra fitness time, or whatever you would prefer to do with that opportunity cost option.

This time factor is worth additional calculation. On average, most Americans work approximately 230 days a year. Therefore, even though both jobs usually require only 50 hours per week at the office, the job in Medium City offers us an extra 34 work days of personal time each year (230 days x 1.5 hours = 345 hours, divided by 10 hours per work day = 34.5 days)!

In addition to the money and time trade-offs of your potential job choices, you might also consider other "quality of life" factors, such as the school systems (when you are a parent), crime rates, museums, zoos, sports teams, and entertainment activities that will match with your single or family lifestyle. You might even develop an MCDM grid (like you did for the Mule and the Dragon) to focus your thoughts on which job or city priorities you favor the most. Would one priority be as dominant as gas mileage was for your car? Would a single factor, such as one job offering promotions earlier, or one city being closer to your parents as you prepare to raise children, be the major determining factor?

Regardless of the job that you select, you will probably want to add a S.M.A.R.T. goal as you "Now act" and accept the job. You might choose a goal such as "I will end every day of my first month at work by asking my boss 'Is there anything else I can do to help before I go home?'" This simple, specific goal might signal your *effort* to your boss, as well as your *ability* to help others, and not just look out for yourself. You might also add a more relaxed S.M.A.R.T. goal, such as "I will try this job (and the accompanying city, lifestyle, etc.) for one year, and if it offers me _____ (a promotion, security, adventure…fill in your specific words), then I will continue working at this job."

After you have been working at the job for a while, you might consider looking at the job with a "timely" life review. Maybe the current job is not ideal, but it serves as a building block toward your long term, *Autoscop*-like identity. For example, in preparation for being a future leader, you might choose to perform as either a salesperson or a teacher for a few years, so that you can deliberately practice and improve your speaking and presentation skills. Alternatively, you might deliberately choose to work at different jobs within the same industry during your 20s (perhaps clothing stores, or restaurants) so that you may develop the hands-on, "street smarts" to one day start your own business.

Additionally, as you look back on your job choices, remember to critique your decision and your POINT analysis abilities, but be more relaxed when you evaluate the outcome. Outcomes can occasionally turn bad, for reasons that you could <u>not</u> control. For example, perhaps you chose the job in Big City, and the pleasant boss that recruited you (the dominant reason that you joined) unexpectedly leaves for another company. As you result, you now work for a boss that seems to lack skill in interacting with people. Although your <u>present</u> <u>situation</u> is not ideal, the <u>past</u> <u>POINT</u> <u>decision</u> that brought you to that job might still have been a good one. What you could control was how you made that decision. If you can review a past decision (and outcome) and say, "Given what I knew back then, I controlled what I could control, and it was a good decision," then you will feel more comfortable with the outcome (even as you learn about what factors you might have failed to calculate).

Finally, as you consider your future outlook, remember the "sunk cost" bias—the past has passed. Looking forward, what can you do in your current position to grow your skills and abilities? Learning such actions in the "now" will help you in the future, in case you need to escape a lousy boss or a lousy job. By POINTing your focus forward in time, you can visualize how to earn a promotion within your company as well as how to be competitive enough for another company to hire you. If today's actions in your current job do not help you get to where you want to be in five years, then you might consider trading that job for something else. It all depends on your goals.

*****

Humans possess the greatest intellectual ability on the planet. In order to take advantage of that ability, we must deliberately practice our decision-making process so that we may develop our four control strengths of money, relationships, time, and values. Otherwise, we will become like Captains who, as they go down with their *Life* ship, hear a faint word in the distance—"Checkmate..."

Additional Principles:

Three Wise Questions
P.O.I.N.T.
Causality
S.M.A.R.T. Goals

For Further Reflection:

1) How might you use The Three Wise questions (or Five, or Seven) to answer the following "problems":

I do not have a romantic partner in my life.
I do not have as much money as I would like.
I do not has as much personal time as I would like.
I do not live the values that I would like.

2) What "causes" you to be happy? Fulfilled? How do these factors meet the three conditions for causality?

3) Would you rather have the certainty of $80, or the uncertain potential of the "coin flip gift?" How does your answer compare with your friends and family?

4) For which of the following decisions would you try to "optimize?"

Marriage, Career, Shoes, Religion, Clothes, Election Knowledge, Entertainment? What would your MCDM calculations look like?

5) What would you say is your ultimate job objective—"Maximum earnings"? "Fulfilling work?" "Low stress?" "Steady pay?" Other? What would your MCDM of a job look like?

For Further Investigation:

Terminator I, Terminator II, Terminator III, Terminator IV, Terminator: The Sarah Connor Chronicles

http://en.wikipedia.org/wiki/IBM_Deep_Blue (cited 15 Jan 09)

"George Plimpton reflects on Man and the Machine," http://www.research.ibm.com/deepblue/home/may11/interview_1.html, (cited 31 Mar 09)

John Nofsinger, *Psychology of Investing*

Malcolm Gladwell, *Blink*

Barry Schwartz, *The Paradox of Choice*

Marianne Bertrand and Sendhil Mullainathan, *"Are Emily and Greg More Employable Than Lakisha and Jamal? : A Field Experiment on Labor Market Discrimination;"*; Working paper series WP 03-22.; Massachusetts Institute of Technology Dept. of Economics, 2003.
   http://papers.ssrn.com/sol3/papers.cfm?abstract_id=422902

Claudia Goldin and Cecilia Rouse. "Orchestrating Impartiality: The Impact Of 'Blind' Auditions On Female Musicians," American Economic Review, 2000, v90.

David Bassett, John Pucher, Ralph Buehler, Dixie Thompson, Scott Crouter, "Walking, Cycling, and Obesity Rates in Europe, North America, and Australia" *Journal of Physical Activity and Health*, November 2008.

Steven Levitt and Stephen Dubner, *Freakonomics*

Blaise Pascal, *Thoughts on Religion*

Rene Descartes, *Meditations of First Philosophy*

For city cost comparisons, see
http://cgi.money.cnn.com/tools/costofliving/costofliving.html, "How far will my salary go in another city?" (cited 31 Mar 09)

Peter Drucker, *The Practice of Management*

Nassim Taleb, *The Black Swan*

John Doullaird, *Mind, Body, and Sport*

Communication: Persuasion beyond Words

The verbal words account for only 7 percent of the meaning in a spoken message. – 1967 UCLA study.

A female student of mine asked, "How long should a woman wait before she engages in intercourse with a man?" After I recovered from the initial shock of her question, my student explained that her fashion-and-gossip magazine had posed that question, as well as offered an answer. Intrigued, I invited the student to join me in examining the magazine article for its persuasiveness. We agreed to use the following communication model, so that we would have common reference for discussing our biases:

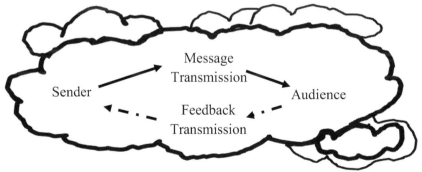

Figure 7-1: Basic Communication Exchange

Figure 7-1 displays a basic communication exchange. It begins with a sender, who attempts to transmit a message to an <u>intended</u> audience. The audience, whether one person or one thousand people, receives some form of that message. Depending on the type of interaction, the audience may then provide feedback to the sender about what was understood—that feedback may come in the form of comments, facial expressions, or disinterest.

Additionally, all communication exchanges are constantly distorted by a "cloud of interference." These distortions occur because of individual factors (e.g., lack of sleep and attentiveness, personal biases) as well as environmental factors (e.g., poorly written e-mail, bad cell phone connection). If you, as a sender, hope to communicate persuasively, then you must be aware of how these communication elements work together.

In this chapter, we shall explore methods and techniques that increase, or decrease, the persuasiveness of a message. We will then apply these concepts as we analyze the article "How long should a woman wait before she engages in intercourse with a guy?" For reasons of anonymity, the specific magazine title and the author's name associated with this real-life scenario have been changed—it seems unfair to single out one "sender" of sexual advice when there are so many magazines and websites that "answer" the "when should you participate in sex" question. Following this analysis, we will conclude the chapter by investigating how the same principles of communication may be applied when you attempt to purchase a car—we will purchase the Dragon vehicle from the last chapter. We begin our analysis by starting with each communication's source—the sender.

The Sender

Whether you are the leader of a group, an equal among peers, or a subordinate to a boss, when you transmit your message (verbally, digitally, or in written form) you as the sender have the ability to influence the persuasiveness of your message. Research on power and influence by scientists such as Bertram Raven, John French, and Gary Yukl suggests that two types of influence techniques—expertise and referent power—are used by people who are more effective as leaders. Let us consider how these two techniques might enhance the persuasion of your message.

Your expertise is derived from your possession of specialized knowledge that few (or possibly no one) among your audience possesses. Expertise can appear in many forms, ranging from an internal knowledge of abstract scientific models to external, "hands on" abilities such as automobile maintenance skills. Sometimes expertise is subtle in nature. For example,

"Hollywood insiders" are valued because they are experts at taking a proposed movie script, networking that script among the right decision-makers, and creating a full movie production deal. Although they get little, if any, mention within a film's closing credits, without their subtle, "behind the scenes" expertise, many movies would not be made.

Your expertise is also more influential if people want to know what you know. For example, a person may be an expert in Star Trek trivia knowledge, but unless that person is at a Star Trek convention, or meeting with fellow Trek-ies, possessing this knowledge may not impress or persuade other people.

Sometimes people attempt to display their expertise by quoting "facts." WARNING: This approach can be dangerous. For example, the overview quote for this chapter references a 1967 study and implies that words account for only seven percent of the meaning of a communication exchange. As David Lapakko has pointed out, this study has been widely referenced in communication textbooks and by TV personalities who give advice. Unfortunately, many of them have wrongly used this "fact." David personally communicated with one of the scientists of the 1967 study, Albert Mehrabian. Albert noted that the study dealt with a very narrow issue—the "communications of feelings and attitudes." Albert did not examine other communication situations, such as when people debate issues or present mathematical information. With regard to the way people had misused his "feelings and attitudes" findings, Albert asked:

"Suppose I want to tell you that the eraser you are looking for is in the second right-hand drawer of my desk in my third floor office. How could anyone contend that the verbal part of the message is only 7% of the message?"

Despite Albert's compelling logic, David uncovered many references and quotes about Albert's studies that explained his results incorrectly. David searched Google using the phrase "communication 93 percent nonverbal." After examining the first 79 websites that referenced communication as being 93 percent nonverbal, David noted that 75 of the websites "simply passed along the numbers as being implicitly correct." Very few websites made the important distinction that the "7% of the message" comment referred to the communication gap between words and feelings, versus other communication possibilities such as the relaying of facts. David suggested that it was highly unlikely that any of the incorrect senders of information had actually read the 1967 study that was referenced. Apparently, repeating a "fact" can be much like the high school practice of "I heard from a friend of a friend that...". Whenever you attempt to send a fact, be sure that you have verified your claims, or at least include a disclaimer such as, "I have not verified this fact yet, but _____ ("the news," "my work mate," "the radio DJ this morning," choose your term) said..."

Besides using expertise, another way to improve the persuasiveness of your message is to develop your referent power—your personal attractiveness to others that is largely based upon your personality and experiences. For example, businesses try to capitalize on the referent power of Hollywood celebrities every year at the Academy Awards ceremonies. The presenters and performers at the Awards typically receive a "goody bag" of items full of the latest gadgets, restaurant certificates, and more. Businesses donate their products to the goody bags hoping that a celebrity will be seen using their product, and that the celebrity's popularity will create a greater demand for the product. A similar undertaking occurs when athletes are courted to endorse shoes, sports drinks, and other products. On a related note, portions of celebrity-like influence can also be gained by non-celebrities if they appear to be physically "beautiful" to others, as research by Daniel Hamermesh and Jeff Biddle has suggested.

Although we may not achieve celebrity status, we may create a more influential persona through our longer-term, *Autoscop*-like identity of accomplishments. Consider the reputation of Colin Powell. Prior to 1996, Colin had served America as its National Security Advisor as well as its Chairman of the Joint Chiefs of Staff (the highest military position possible) during the military operations of Desert Shield and Desert Storm. His character and accomplishments were so impressive that polls showed him as being able to defeat the President of that time—Bill Clinton—during the 1996 Presidential election.

With regard to personality, Colin wrote in his book *My American Journey* that "Perpetual optimism is a force multiplier"—"force multiplier" implies that you and your teammates (whether the teammates are within work groups, sports teams, family, or friends) are able to accomplish more when you conduct yourself, as well as send your messages, with optimism. I believe that Colin was too humble about how his abilities and accomplishments supported his optimism. Colin's optimism was a force multiplier in part because Colin's consistent, intentional, and excellent performances had shown that he could be trusted by his bosses, peers, and subordinates. Alternatively, if Colin had been an optimistic fool who was not effective at accomplishing his various jobs and missions, he would not have been entrusted with so many important positions, and his referent power would have been minimal. Reputation matters. Colin was later selected to serve as America's 65th Secretary of State—arguably the second most powerful position in American politics.

The Message

One of my favorite teachers offered me a basic formula for designing persuasive messages that would help change a person's behavior. He said that a message would be more persuasive if it contained four elements:

1. Historical references.
2. Common goals and visions for the future.
3. A justification of why the current moment—"now"—is so important.
4. KISS: "Keep It Simple, Stupid!"

...why might this be? Let us briefly consider each point...

The first factor—history—helps highlight your expertise and referent power. When your audience (whether your romantic partner, a group of co-workers, or a group of strangers) is able to believe that you have a good understanding of them and their history, your power of persuasion increases. Consider how politicians try to "connect" with voters. For example, during one of the 2008 Presidential debates, Barack Obama and John McCain referred to a person known as "Joe the Plumber" over 20 times in an attempt to show that they understood how a middle-income American lived and felt.

In addition to using past events and situations to connect with an audience, senders acquire greater message persuasiveness when they are able to richly describe future goals and destinations. Consider what happens when you go car shopping. If you are reasonably serious about buying a certain car (to the point where the car salesman has run a credit check on you), it is quite possible that the car salesman will offer you the opportunity to "take it for a test drive" so that you can feel how real it would be to own the car. The salesman may even say, "Why don't you take this home tonight, and if you don't want it in the morning, feel free to bring it back." Salespeople know that the more they can make the vision of ownership become a reality for you, the more likely you are to buy their car. We will have more to say about the car buying experience in a few pages.

For interesting insights into the art of persuasive communication, consider reading Gerry Spence's *How to Argue and Win Every Time*. Gerry is an internationally-renowned attorney who (as his *Trial Lawyer College* website noted at the time of this writing):

1. Has never lost a criminal case as a prosecutor or a defense attorney.
2. Has not lost a civil case since 1969.
3. Has had more multi-million dollar verdicts without an intervening loss than any lawyer in America.

Gerry offers impressive expertise credentials, and I believe that you would place him, Burton Malkiel (Chapter 2), and David Buss (Chapter 3) as credible experts in their fields who offer valuable insights that you may wish to act upon.

Another way to make your messages more persuasive is to include a reason with your requests, as a study by Ellen Langer and her colleagues showed. During their "experiment," Ellen and her colleagues asked people to attempt to step in front of others already at a copier machine, and then make use of the copier machine. Some of Ellen's "out of order" people asked the next-in-line person if they could make a copy. Other people asked to go first and also included a reason, such as "because I am in a rush," or even "…because I have to make copies." The result? People were much more effective at interrupting the line order when they included a reason (over 90 percent successful line-cutting ability, versus 60 percent when no reason was given). Perhaps offering a reason prevents the other person from feeling like they are being disrespected or bullied? Whatever the cause-and-effect relationship, it appears to be useful to offer a reason for your requests. If you frequently offer reasons, then on those rare occasions when you are in a rush, and can only say "Would you please do this? I will explain why later…" your reputation for being reasonable will provide support for your request.

As you form your persuasive messages, you might want to consider the "focus" of your message—is it positive, or negative? For example, a S.M.A.R.T. goal typically has a proactive focus. You do not make a goal such as "I will not become fired." Instead, you use a growth focus, such as "I will achieve a promotion." Focusing a message can be difficult. For example, I have noticed a number of teachers and instructors who innocently use phrases such as "Don't forget that you have a test during the next class." Innocently enough, the teachers reference the focused action of "forget." The instructors are inadvertently saying that they view the students as people who forget things, so "don't do your negative behavior." In contrast, other instructors say "Kindly remember that you have a test during the next class." Such a statement focuses on the positive abilities of the students to "remember." The underlying tone is optimistic and praising, versus unintentionally distrusting of people's forgetfulness.

Similarly, if you have ever been responsible for young children, you already know the importance of properly focused words. For example, if you and a child are getting out of vehicle at a mall parking lot, you probably would not say "Don't wander off while I grab my things," because there is too much uncertainty about how the child will interpret "don't wander off." Does "wander" mean "more than 3 feet?" The next car over? Two cars? In contrast, if you say "Keep your hand on the car," assuming that the child complies, you can be reasonably certain that the child will stay close enough to that car so that other cars could not hit the child, nor could strangers be able to grab the child.

This positive focus technique also works well on adults. I was once teaching this concept at a police academy. As we discussed the power of stereotypes and positively worded messages, we realized that when the police have a suspect within their sight, the police do not say, "Do not move around," or, "Do not heat up!" Instead, the police say, (all together now) "FREEZE!"

Telling people what to positively accomplish, instead of referencing what they should avoid, can impact a person's focus. Perhaps that is why political groups choose names such as "Pro-Life" and "Pro-Choice"—it feels less powerful if you are simply "Anti-Life," or "Anti-anything" for that matter. You might consider experimenting with this technique (versus "Don't take my word for it"). Ed Oakly and Dough Krug provide further elaborations about this "positive message" technique in their book, *Enlightened Leadership: Getting to the Heart of Change.*

A third component of persuasion—justifying the importance of "now"—helps convey the sense of urgency surrounding your actions and decisions. If you really want to change someone's behavior, you need to convince them that your issue cannot wait any longer to be resolved—it needs action now! Consider some of the classic speeches associated with America's growth in social and race relations. When Martin Luther King Jr. delivered his "I Have a Dream" speech, he used the phrase "Now is the time" multiple times as he proclaimed his vision and the need for people to take a stand for equality and justice. 40 years later, Bill Cosby's "Pound Cake Speech" used the phrase "It's our time" multiple times as he highlighted how parents—and not just government policies (such as the end of segregation)—strongly impact the growth of children right now. "Now" is the decisive moment. "Now" conveys that this moment can change the outcome of events. "Now," not later.

Additionally, when you choose to emphasize the importance of "now," which do you think would be better to emphasize: what your audience will currently gain from a situation, or what your audience will lose from a situation? If you really want to grab someone's attention, research by Nobel Prize winners Daniel Kahneman and Amos Tversky would suggest that you should emphasize what will be lost. For example, consider the following:

Suppose that, one afternoon, you walk out to your mailbox and you find a card from your grandma. She has sent you a card that contains a $50 bill and her wish for you to "just go spend this on something that will make you happier." In general, it would be natural if you were to be happier as a result of this event. On a scale of 1 to 10, you might be a "+3" as a result of the experience (maybe you are a "+2," or a "+4," but the general idea is that you are happier).

Now, reset your mind, and pretend that the mailbox scenario never happened. Instead, imagine that you are at a restaurant with a romantic partner, and the waiter has just handed you the bill. After considering the tip, it looks as though you will have to pay $50 for the experience. You perceive this price to be an amusing coincidence because you have a $50 bill in your money clip (or wallet, or purse). As you look within your money holder, you suddenly realize that your $50 bill is missing. Since you have a credit card, you are able to pay for the meal, but you are still confused about where you put that $50. When you arrive home that night, you look around the table, underneath the furniture, and within the clothes that you have worn during the last two days. No $50 bill is found.

You are now upset. Most likely, on a scale of -1 to -10, you will feel something close to a "-6" (assuming that you were a "+3" when you were sent the $50 of surprise money). Individual responses will vary, of course, but an "average" negative response from people losing something that they value is nearly twice as strong as their positive feelings that they gain from something of equal value. Losses affect us more than gains.

Using "loss" to motivate a behavior change can be found within some of the "intervention" techniques associated with trying to rehabilitate a drug addict. Among the many steps involved with an intervention, one technique includes having a group of people respected by the addict write down all of the negative consequences that the addicted individual's actions have caused. They then write down what will be lost if that person continues their addiction actions. The document of compiled losses is then read aloud to the addict in an attempt to persuade them to change. This increased awareness of loss can be quite motivating.

The fourth condition of a persuasive message is that it meets the principle of K.I.S.S.—"Keep it simple, Stupid!" Although it sounds rather harsh, the K.I.S.S. approach reminds us, somewhat amusingly, of the importance of keeping our messages focused on a few main themes. Too many ideas sent at one time can become an information overload. Examples of reducing overload can be found in school textbooks. Most textbooks are broken up into chapters, and then by topics, and then even further by sub-topics. Two (non-textbook) message techniques that can help keep your messages simple are the use of symbols and the repetition of message themes.

The first simplifying tool—symbols—can be found throughout society, such as within religions, government flag designs, and school crests. Message symbols, analogies, and metaphors can help solidify an idea. The famous "I Have a Dream" speech does not reference "justice" and "segregation" as abstract, philosophical concepts. Martin Luther King Jr. spoke of these ideas in terms of money—symbols to which people could easily relate. He noted how the civil rights movement was designed to "cash a check" and how America had "defaulted" on that "promissory note." He further used money symbols to note that people had been given a "bad check" when it came to such justice—the check had "insufficient funds." Ultimately, he did not believe that the "bank of justice" was "bankrupt." Consider watching (and re-watching) this symbol filled, nation-altering, speech for its use of persuasive techniques.

The other message simplification tool—the constant repetition of a theme—follows an old piece of communication advice: "Tell the audience what you want to tell them (use an overview), tell the audience what you wanted to tell them (the main portion of the message), and then tell the audience what you told them (provide a brief review)." Even when there are only 30 seconds or less to send a message, many television and radio advertisements use a slogan, a jingle, or a symbol during every commercial to leave you with a reminder of them. Is this repetition technique effective?

- Which shoe company has used the slogan "Just do it?"
- Which technology company is named after a piece of fruit?
- What product suggested "If you don't look good, we don't look good?"

If you could provide answers to two or three of these questions, you now have evidence of the effectiveness of repetition.

Once you are acquainted with the four major components of a convincing message, you can deliberately practice these persuasion techniques. I often ask my students to give an impromptu speech based upon the four components. For example, if one of the students plays sports, then I might say to the student, "Congratulations, you are now your team's captain. Your team has made the playoffs, and it is four days until the opening game. You are getting ready to start practice. What will you say to motivate your team through practice?" It is interesting to watch how the students will look to the classroom board (I might have written something like "past," "future," "now," and "KISS" on the board), begin speaking, and slowly pick up momentum as they work their way through the various stages of their speech. Within five minutes, they have usually assembled a pretty respectable message of motivation. Such persuasively formatted messages can be effective during work, family, and other relationship communications.

The Audience

"Know your audience" is generally good advice when it comes to composing and transmitting a message. It seems likely that people will receive the exact same message differently based upon their level of wealth, their gender, their level of hurriedness, and their religious orientation (to name just a few of the money, relationship, time and values biases). In addition to all of these considerations, one more technique seems worth considering—the vocabulary level of your message. As discussed in the sender portion of the communication process, being able to establish a good relationship with your audience can strengthen your referent power and your ability to persuade and influence. Using the wrong vocabulary can weaken your relationship.

For example, consider how some groups of people have a shared vocabulary, jargon, or slang associated with their group. Sometimes an inner, almost secret vocabulary is developed within the group because it helps transmit long, descriptive information in a brief and concise manner.

This saves time because everyone in the <u>intended</u> audience knows what the terms mean. Those who are able to speak the lingo effectively also reflect their expert power. For example, fighter pilots may use words such as "tally," "visual," "blind," "no joy," "bingo," and "joker" to discuss various mission situation factors. Similarly, Scientists may use words like "endogeneity" and "heteroskadasticity" to discuss research concerns. Knowing whether an audience is more comfortable with a word such as "ubiquitous" or "everywhere" can be the difference between transmitting a stilted communiqué or transmitting a persuasive message.

Feedback

If you design a message to discuss a few main themes, then it will necessarily leave out other, less important, pieces of information. After you have transmitted a message, you may be left wondering "Did the audience understand what I transmitted?" Therefore, if time permits, you should try to offer the audience a chance to learn more about your message, or topics related to that message. Messages should probably end with "Are there any questions?" or "If you have any questions, feel free to contact me." This allows the audience the chance to ask questions for clarity.

Similarly, there are some other messages where you want to ensure that the audience understood your intent. For example, you may need a friend to give you a ride to work. You want to be sure that you and your friend both agree on the time and place of your meeting. After you finish stating what time you would like to be picked up, in a perfect world your friend would automatically start saying, "Ok, I think I heard you correctly. Let me see, you said that…" Alternatively, you might need to prompt your friend for the feedback. Avoid asking, "Did you get all of that?"—that is too general of a question. It leaves open the possibility that a person can answer "Yes" without actually demonstrating that they understood the important details. Instead, you might ask "Would you please repeat, or at least loosely paraphrase, what I just said?" If you want to seem more humble about it, you could offer a leading sentence of "…just to be sure I said what I think I said, because I'm sleepy today, would you please repeat back what you heard?"

When you are the audience, and a person transmits a message to you, you can respond in a number of ways. The best responses usually begin by using a form of "message reciprocity"—you tell the sender what you have heard, summarizing the key points of their original message. In contrast, one of the worst feedback actions is to ignore the sender's message. As an extreme example, can you imagine how a woman would feel if she told her husband that she was pregnant, and he said nothing except "So, you don't know if it is going to rain today?" Being disconnected from a message leads to the loss of your persuasive referent and expert powers, whether as the audience or the sender. Similarly, being aware of your non-verbal gestures (e.g., yawning, poor eye contact, posture) and your communication partner's gestures will improve your ability to understand whether the messages are generating interest and motivation. Although I do not have a favorite body language book, I do recommend that people study the subtle use and persuasion that body postures and facial expressions can provide.

As an audience member, you can even choose to respond to a sender with a (polite) disagreement about parts of their message, and the messenger will still feel as though you were paying attention. Disagreements, and the possible apologies that may be necessary as a result, deserve a bit more elaboration. Thus...

Tough Communication: Disagreements and Apologies

Sometimes people just disagree. That does not mean that both sides are right, but it does mean that their communication may be at a stalemate. From experience, I believe that you should save the phrase "You are wrong" for only the most extreme circumstances, and only in the most black and white, provable situations (such as elementary school math problems). "You are wrong" can easily be perceived by a communication partner as a personal attack on them and their intelligence. Occasionally, you may want that effect.

However, in most communication situations people are interested in evaluating the ideas within a message, and not evaluating the person who said the ideas. Even when people try to relate (poorly) by using referent language such as, "I know how you feel, but you are wrong...", they risk damaging their relationship with the other person. Besides, rarely, if ever, can one person know exactly how another "feels"—that is a tough phrase to authentically say. In general, avoid beginning any discussion with the phrase "I know how you feel...."

Your communication relationships will likely benefit from using the following, less aggressive statements. Consider using phrases such as, "I think I understand where you are coming from (and perhaps include some message reciprocity). At the same time, I think there are some additional factors that are influencing my perspective…" I have found the phrase "At the same time" to be much less confrontational than "You are wrong" or "but" or "however."

Occasionally, I have been given a chance to exercise these techniques within emotionally charged debates. One of the most contentious debates was concerned with whether or not homosexual behaviors should be allowed in the US military. At the time of my debates, military members were not allowed to engage in homosexual acts. Many individuals engaged in the verbal and written debates surrounding the question "Should the US military allow homosexual behaviors?" Within these debates I used or experienced various strategies for disagreeing with others and their alternative (and occasionally "opposite") views. Six of the most common persuasion techniques were:

#1. Use principle-centered logic.
#2. Show the other person's "incomplete logic."
#3. Investigate the other person's causal claims.
#4. Introduce additional evidence.
#5. Use credible analogies.
#6. Be civil, and avoid "argumentum ad hominem" tactics (attacking the other person, when you should instead be analyzing the issues and the logic of their claims).

I believed that the American military should preserve its principled practice (technique #1) and continue its policy of "separate sexual preferences in areas of close body contact." More specifically, the United States' military had previously separated men and women from each other in bathrooms, bedrooms, and locker rooms. This avoided unnecessary risks and disruptions to military operations. Allowing homosexual behaviors would ignore this principle and create an exception for homosexuals. As could be expected, gay advocacy individuals disagreed with my position. You may view their opinions, and others, at *The New York Times* "Room for Debate" website, in the forum titled "In the Barracks, Out of the Closet."

Sometimes, gay advocates said to me "Gays are fully capable of serving in the military." I responded to their statements using guiding principle #2— demonstrate incomplete logic—the biggest challenges to the American military were not concerned with a homosexual's ability.

For example, I asked audiences to consider why the American military did not allow swimsuit calendars in its workplaces. This allowed us to discuss how passive paper objects could negatively affect the morale of female military members (NATO and other European military environments may have differed). Besides calendars, the American military did not allow male behavior that might reduce female morale. For example, if a male were to use a female's bathroom, locker room, or bedroom—even if he had no aggressive intentions toward any females who might also be using those facilities—an investigation against him would be generated.

This raised a question related to "hostile work environment" concerns: if the morale of a heterosexual female military member could be negatively affected by a passive object such as a calendar, or a behavior from a male who had no aggressive interest in her, then would her discomfort any less valid if it were caused by being required to constantly share close-body-proximity facilities with a Lesbian who had no aggressive interest in her?

I also asked listeners to extend this thought experiment further—let us insert the phrase "married man" for "Lesbian" and reconsider the question. Should the military have allowed married men to share showers with females? Married men should have no aggressive interests in women, even though they do have the same sexual preferences as Lesbians. However, to avoid unnecessary disruptions to operations, the military still had not integrated sexual preferences. There did not appear to be a logical answer to how the military could easily combine sexual preferences.

Instead, the military's heterosexually-biased policy mirrored the policies of non-military organizations, such as when airport authorities physically searched passengers using agents of the same gender, or when businesses and public schools separated bathrooms and gym lockers by gender. In contrast, an openly gay military that removed the anonymity of sexual preferences appeared to be the heterosexual equivalent of requiring females to constantly share bathrooms, locker rooms, and bedrooms with males. Combining sexual preferences (i.e., open Lesbians with heterosexual women) would challenge American commanders with privacy violations and dignity infractions that would unnecessarily reduce unit effectiveness.

Thus, from my perspective, this was not an issue about an individual's capability—it was an issue about how military members' sexual preferences affected one another. The gay capability claims were not the concern.

Technique #3—investigating a person's causal claims—can also be necessary during a discussion or debate. For example, one argument from a gay advocacy book referenced a Zogby poll from the year 2006 and its questions about how the behavior of homosexuals (who had not been separated from the military) affected morale. The author stated, "Tellingly, of those who knew of gays in their unit, the overwhelming majority stated that their presence had little or no impact on the unit's morale." The author did not offer a reader the actual table of the responses, just his interpretation of that table.

Here is a condensed chart from that poll, questions 20 & 21:

	Personal Morale	Unit Morale
Negative:	28	27
No Impact:	66	64
Positive:	6	3

...the questions were, "How did the presence of known gays or lesbians in your last unit impact your personal morale, and your unit's overall morale?"

There certainly appears to be a negative effect—over 25% of the troops stated that the presence of known gays or lesbians had a **negative** impact on their personal and unit morale. Indeed, the ratios of negative-to-positive impact were 4:1 and 9:1 (28:6 and 27:3, respectively). For consideration, suppose that a Scientist had a bias that "policies and rules should produce benefits" versus "policies and rules should not harm things much." In this case, the evidence of harms appears to outweigh the evidence of benefits. However, by using Lawyer-like advocacy and interpretation, as well as excluding the actual chart, the gay advocacy author presented the evidence as a support for open homosexuality.

An additional historical bias also seemed worth considering. More specifically, the military had not allowed swimsuit calendars in its workplaces, out of respect for the decreased morale and decreased effectiveness that such calendars might cause females (who made up approximately 20% of the military). If the military had traditionally avoided policies that might negatively affect approximately 20% of its members, why would the military adopt a new policy that would create a 27% negative effect on morale (Zogby estimate)? Given that the population of gay military members had been approximated to be around 2.5% (see the estimates by Gary Gates), it appeared that more population harms than benefits would result from open homosexual behaviors within the military—27% vs. 2.5%.

Another claim from gay advocates was that military policies banning homosexual activity caused the loss of millions of dollars of training and skills. To examine this causal claim, we should ask "What if gay service members had never joined the military and been trained?" Would the missions to which they were assigned have still been accomplished? That answer was "Yes," because the military was designed to carry on its mission (via multiple people receiving the same training) so that, in the unfortunate event that someone were killed, or even just sick at the time of the mission, the mission would still be accomplished. The cause of lost skills had not been the homosexual behavior ban. The skills were lost because homosexuals voluntarily entered the military, accepted training, and then did not honor their oath. Had they never joined the military, then their training would have been allocated to heterosexuals who would not have dishonored their oath via homosexual behavior.

Another way to respectfully disagree with someone is to "introduce new evidence" (technique #4). Although concerns of male rape were one possible topic, I tended to rely on reports about men who are sexual with men (MSM) from the Centers for Disease Control and Prevention (CDC). For example, the CDC had reported that even though only approximately 4 percent of men in the United States engage in MSM behaviors, the rate of new HIV diagnoses among MSM in the United States was more than 44 times that of other men. Evidence such as this suggested that the US endorsement of MSM behavior would lead to an increase in the number of military members acquiring HIV. Once a military member contracted HIV, that member would no longer be deployable, and so military deployment effectiveness would become reduced. Given the reasonable assumption that the military "avoids unnecessary risks" (most military operations are already risky enough), endorsing open homosexual behavior appeared to be a negative, unnecessary risk.

An analogy method (technique #5) further supported the "no homosexual behavior" position. If policy makers learned that they could greatly reduce some "Factor X" from hurting military effectiveness by restricting certain behaviors, would the policy makers create such laws? The answer appeared to be "Yes." For example, military members were constrained—they were not allowed to ride motorcycles unless they wore helmets. By this analogy, it appeared that policy makers had the right to reduce HIV by constraining certain sexual behaviors.

A different analogy that gay advocacy groups claimed was that "Other militaries are openly gay, so why not the US?" One response to this type of foreign military comparison was reminiscent of our preschool learning—our parents and teachers would issue warnings of "Just because Skippy jumps off the bridge does not mean that you should too." Using other, non-superpower nations as a basis for telling the US how to run its military was like using a high school football team's playbook for a professional NFL team. Other nations had significantly smaller militaries and military roles. They also belonged to nations whose cultural values greatly differed from American culture (e.g., legalized civilian prostitution, topless beaches, and mandatory military service). These nations were not apples-to-apples comparisons, or in the more technical language of a Scientist, these comparisons were not "externally valid." When an analogy requires too great of a leap of logic, it is no longer persuasive.

One other tactic, which was used by gay advocates against those with the "no homosexual behavior" perspective, was the "argumentum ad hominem." This version of "name calling" did nothing to inform the debated issue. For example, in that gay advocacy book I mentioned earlier, the author stereotyped me and other military members when he wrote, "The culture of the military throughout the 1990s—largely unchanged from previous decades—was one that lazily exploited anti-gay and anti-female sentiment to bolster feelings of male vigor and machismo that were, for centuries, felt to be central to warrior success." Additionally, he wrote (and I have added the underlined emphasis), "Equally important is the ethical question of how many homophobes have to come around before a nation is allowed to do the right thing?" as well as "The gay ban is no less than the stalling of the march toward Enlightenment..." He also referred to those with a differing opinion as "morally and intellectually bankrupt."

Given that these claims were both value-based and, if true, rather damaging, we should consider whether the gay advocacy author had actually applied morality & Enlightenment principles.

To answer this question, we might consider where morality and ethics come from, and what conclusions we would reach as a result. For example, if morality is based upon personal opinion, then judgments are simply differing opinions of relativity, with no absolute Truth. If this is the standard for morality, then this gay author should have written that "I may not understand or agree with the military culture and its ban on homosexual behavior, but I must respect its relatively unique and effective culture." Individual relativism does not support gay behavior as the "correct" or "enlightened" Truth. The gay advocate would have lost persuasion by using this values approach.

Alternatively, perhaps the gay advocate was claiming that morality and ethics come from group consensus? If that were the standard, then the U.S. democracy had already formed a consensus via the U.S. Congressional statement that homosexual acts "create an unacceptable risk to the morale, good order, discipline, and unit cohesion that are the essences of military capability" (a direct quote from Section 654 of the US Code of Law). Group consensus did not support gay behavior as "the right thing." The gay author would have lost his persuasion by using this values approach.

One other appeal to morality and ethics might have been to use a higher source of wisdom, such as the Judaic, Christian, or Muslim religions. If these traditions were the standard, then such higher wisdom did not support gay behavior—by military members or anyone else. The gay advocate would have lost persuasion by using this values approach.

Although there was tremendous disagreement and emotion surrounding the policy of allowing homosexual behavior in the military, in late 2010 a coalition of gay advocacy stakeholders were able to pass a bill which repealed the ban on homosexual behavior in the US military. There does not appear to be major evidence that either side of the debate was ever persuaded by the other.

As was written at the beginning of this section, sometimes people just disagree. If you have disagreed with someone, then your most likely next step is to clarify all of the assumptions associated with each side of the issue. If, after reviewing each other's assumptions and evidence, no one budges, and no new information is available, is there really any benefit gained by continuing to discuss, debate or argue? If you are defending your religion, your family honor, or some other highly valued issue, then perhaps it is. Otherwise, we must consider how much of an opportunity cost we are paying by continuing to debate an issue with another person. The effort may not be worth it. Over the course of your *Life*, you will have to prioritize which "battles" you are willing to fight with your energies. You may not always win. Some people will probably not like you and disparage you. At the same time, waging principled battles will support your W.C.M.J. growth.

On a more daily basis, as none of us are perfect, it seems inevitable that occasionally people will hurt each other during a debate or some other interaction, whether by accident or by design. Sometimes an offender will say, "I'm sorry," and feel that this is sufficient. From a persuasion perspective, an offender can go farther by asking, "Will you forgive me?" Such a question gives the power to resolve the incident to the person who was hurt. Some people are, understandably, uncomfortable with giving away such power because their egos do not want to admit that they were wrong. A person can even state that they were wrong, but if the tone of their message is not sincere enough, then they will still have troubles—just ask Bill Clinton.

In August of 1998, while he was President, he delivered a speech about how he had cheated on his wife with the White House intern Monica Lewinsky. In what appeared to be a reaction to his inability to say "I'm sorry" during that 1998 speech, Bill had to deliver more speeches, until he ultimately said that he was "profoundly sorry" in December, 1998.

Perhaps if Bill had followed the advice of certain communication traditions he would have only needed to apologize once. These traditions require that an apology have three parts:

1. The person states what they did wrong.
2. The person states that they are sorry (or asks for forgiveness).
3. The person offers to make amends (i.e., if they broke your toy, they offer to replace it).

Using this three-part communication technique can help restore relationships more rapidly, regardless of who or how someone was hurt.

One last piece of communication advice seems prudent—only write, say, or act as though everyone will eventually learn what you have been doing. Stated differently, consider only speaking and acting in ways that you would be willing to publicly repeat to anyone else. Most likely, you already know who are your trusted confidants. However, occasionally one of them forwards an e-mail, or repeats a message to someone that you did not intend to receive the message. If you only act as if everyone will know what you have done, you will not ever be embarrassed or compromised by what you have written, said, or done (i.e., a ranting e-mail intended to blow off steam).

Over time, the communication techniques that we have been exploring, when combined with the principles from the previous chapters, will help provide you with the insight to see through superficial persuasion.

Armed with these techniques, my female student and I began to analyze:

"How long should a woman wait before she engages in intercourse with a man?"

Having discussed the various parts of the communication process, the student and I began to consider the sex article's persuasiveness by looking for clues about the credibility of its sender. First, we looked for the author's expertise. The subtitle of the article claimed that the author (a man) was a "relationship expert." Hmmm…"relationship expert?" Really? Neither the student nor I saw any references about the author's relationship expertise. We did not see any "book smarts" credentials, such as a Master's degree, or Ph.D. earned in a social science field such as psychology or anthropology. Nor did we see any "street smarts" references of experience, such as a claim that he had been in a happily committed relationship for over 5 years, or that he had been sought out by thousands of couples for relationship counseling.

We also did not see the author use any evidence within the article—there was no basis for his conclusion. By the end of the article, we believed that this expert advice was merely some guy's opinion, which seemed odd because "he" was not a "she"—could he really give advice about how she "felt" and should use her body? Could he really relate? Overall, we found neither expert nor referent power influencing us. We were not persuaded.

We also noticed that there was very little "historical connection" to establish rapport with us as readers. This was understandable, because the magazine appears to have over a million readers, so coming up with a significant connection for each and every reader would be difficult. Still, we thought that the article might begin with a loss theme, such as "Engaging in sex too early can destroy a promising relationship." No such luck. In this case, the first sentence of the article began by stating that once a gal meets a guy that she likes, "all she can think about is having sex with him." Really? This seemed rather insulting to my female student, who considered herself to be more cultivated than some primitive, sex-craving, animal.

My female student was the intended audience of the magazine—she was a female between ages 18 and 30. However, she did not feel a strong connection with the author's advice. In fact, when the author used lingo that described relationships as "power plays," my student became both amused and irritated. Why, she wondered, did this author view relationships as a combative game, versus a serious, growth-oriented partnership? Why did the author describe dating in terms of "dating power dynamics" within which women "lose the upper hand" and can "feel helpless?"

Then came the major point of the message—the answer to when a woman should engage in sex with her man. The author pointed out that it was important to delay sex as long as possible—"at least a month." 31 days? My student laughed.

As for me, a male and a parent, I am certain that I was not the intended audience of this writer. Because of the value systems that I have examined, and the systems that I have subsequently chosen to live, I did not connect well with this author's message. Waiting just one month before two people engage in procreative acts seems risky because the guy could be faking affection just to achieve a sexual engagement. Some males can easily fake a good attitude and speak glib statements of commitment for 31 days. If you are a female and you doubt this, find an older brother, or a man who has been married long enough to suggest that he is in a serious commitment, and ask him if he has ever seen other guys fake behaviors of interest enough to impress a woman and win a date, and then "something more." One month is not enough time. Ask your trusted male if he can also recall a time when a female was not suspicious as to why she seemed so worthy of a stranger's attention. Then ask him, "If you had a daughter or a sister, would you be comfortable with her saying that she had conquered all dating dynamics and power plays by waiting 31 days?" As the *Relationships* Chapter highlighted, the evidence suggests that people should, initially, be less sexually engaged if they want lasting, long-term happiness.

Based upon our communication principles, the sex author was not persuasive in selling his 31-day recommendation.

Examining another sales attempt—persuasion during the purchase of a Dragon—concludes our chapter…

Buying the Dragon

When last we left our car shopping experience in Chapter 6, we had completed our POINT decision process at the "If" stage. Let us assume that we have decided to "now act" and purchase the Dragon. Let us now add what we have learned about communication and apply it to a real-life experience, changing some names along the way.

In preparation for buying the "Dragon," I decided to build up my expert power. I recalled that time and diversity were two useful tools for building a good investment strategy. I considered my vehicle to be a significant investment. Although I did not expect this "investment" to result in more money per se, the Dragon would be my primary transportation to work and thus an important component in my wealth-building plan. Having already completed my research on its reliability and safety, and having test driven a Mule and other cars, I decided that I wanted the Dragon, and that I wanted it at a good price.

While researching how to use time to my car-buying advantage, I came across a number of sources that suggested that people should buy a car at the end of each month and at the end of each year (just after Christmas). During these time periods, the auto salespeople usually have a higher self-interest bias to sell a new or used car—companies often offer bonuses or vacations to their sales staff depending upon whether they meet monthly, quarterly, or yearly sales goals. Therefore, at the end of a month, the sales people who are close to meeting their goals may be more willing to deal (and receive a smaller sales commission on your deal) so that they may receive a bigger "total sales" bonus at the end of the time period.

As I did not need the vehicle right away, I used approximately two months to search the web for the various dealerships that sold Dragons. At the same time, I also reviewed websites such as www.edmunds.com, www.kbb.com, and www.cars.com to estimate what would be a good price, by looking at the "invoice" prices. I calculated that the average of the three "invoice" prices from the three websites (($19,720 + 19,430 + 19,140 / 3) = $19,430). I then multiplied that price of $19,430 by 1.05 (to offer the dealer a 5% profit...I do believe that people should be able to make a living). This led me to believe that a fair price for a Dragon would be around $20,400.

Then I remembered that dealerships do not only negotiate on price, they also negotiate on financing. I expected to use a 5-year loan to pay for the Dragon. So I went to a car loan website and started to compute the different prices and interest rates that would be equal to the total amount I would pay if I paid $20,400, with zero percent interest, over 5 years—60 payments (5 years x 12 months per year = 60). Chart 7-2 shows those combinations:

If it Cost	% Interest
$20,400	0
$19,940	0.9
$19,446	1.9
$18,969	2.9
$18,507	3.9
$18,061	4.9
$17,629	5.9

Chart 7-2: Similar Cost & Interest Combinations for 60 months

Having determined the tradeoffs between price and interest rates, I started searching Dragon dealerships. Some websites required that I register my e-mail or phone number in order to look at their website. This allowed them to try to and entice me to visit their lot ("Have I got a deal for you…and only you…if you come in by tomorrow…"). Similarly, after taking a test drive with a sales agent, some agents would be relentless about wanting me to buy their car that day. They would say things such as "What would I need to do for you to be able to take this car home today?" These "limited time" pressure sales tactics were not very attractive.

Eventually, I found a dealer's website that showed a Dragon on the lot with the features I that I wanted for $21,000. I e-mailed the dealership, asking if that Dragon was still on the lot. The internet salesman wrote back "Yes," and asked if he could call me. We talked, and the salesman said that he would make me the "proud owner" of a Dragon.

The next day, I drove up to Dragon-land with my wife and kids. When I arrived, a young looking salesman sat down with me. Since I had already driven a few Dragons, I was ready to see their Dragon and negotiate the price down to around $20,400. I asked the salesman about the price of the Dragon, and the young man said that the price would be "around $24,000."

I rose to leave, and politely said that there must have been a mistake, as I was told that there would be a vehicle with the features that I wanted for around $21,000. The salesman said that such a vehicle had just been sold last night.

"Really?" I replied. I thanked him for his time, and my family and I started walking.

The young salesman looked surprised. He hastily said "Wait here for a second, please!" and he went off to retrieve a different salesman—an older gentleman, this time. By replacing the salesman, I believe that he was hoping for a restart of expertise and referent power. I wondered if the dealership had trained its staff to do this—use the first salesman to try a get a high price from the customer, and if that did not work, switch to a second salesman.

I explained to the older gentleman that I was promised that I would be made a "proud" Dragon owner, and that, right now, I was not feeling very proud of the whole experience. I then informed the gentlemen that I was a teacher of over 100 students every year, and that I would be telling them of the poor treatment that I received at this dealership.

Now I was using my referent power. I did not scream. I spoke calmly, but the gentleman could tell that a bad relationship and reputation had been formed. Also, I flexed my expert power by telling him about other sales lots that were offering that same vehicle he was offering at $23,835 for $21,500.

He looked reflective. Then he said. "I'll be right back." 10 minutes later, he said, "We do have one other model that we are driving over from our other lot across town. It has more features than you wanted, but we can 'give' it to you for $20,500."

Was it really being driven across town, or was it a tactic that was developed to keep me at the dealership? I could not be certain. Lacking any certainty, I informed him that my experience had been so irritating that even a good deal of $20,500 no longer looked good.

So he asked, "What would be a good deal, Dr. Maue?"

I told him that I had not yet secured financing, so I asked if he could find me 0% financing. He left again for another 10 minutes. Then he came back with two offers:

      a) $20,500 with a 0% car loan rate
      b) $18,000 with a 3.5% car loan rate

I looked at my piece of paper (I had placed a miniature Chart 7-2 in my pocket) and was quickly able to deduce that the $18,000 offer with 3.5% financing was the better deal. We agreed on the amounts and then he sent me to one more person—the Finance & Warranty Guy.

The F&W Guy said that he could lower my payments and extend my warranty from three to five years. This seemed odd to me. How was this possible?

"I can do it," he began, "by 'giving' you a six-year loan. I…"

"No thank you."

"But…"

"No thank you."

And so, compared to the MSRP of $23,835, $18,000 felt rather satisfying. It was $5,800 lower than the MSRP (MSRP stands for Manufacturer's Suggested Retail Price), or approximately $3,335 lower if you consider the interest impacts.

So, for about 15 hours of pre-work (internet searches and test drives while not in a hurry), I built up my expertise and saved around $3,335. That was like earning $222 per hour to do car research. Expert and referent power had paid off. So, too, had my willingness to walk away from a bad deal.

One last short story: I have a friend who did some pre-research on a Dragon, and then began calling all of the reasonably close dealerships (2 hours or less drive) that were in the area, asking for a significantly low price. He began each call by saying "Hi, I have already test driven a Dragon, and if you have one on the lot with the right features for $17,000, I will make it worth your 30 minutes of paperwork time by adding another sale to your monthly record." On the tenth dealership call, he received the deal that he wanted!

*****

Whether sorting out sexual decisions with your most intimate partner, or negotiating against an intellectual stranger, you may use the components of communication to persuasively impact the outcomes. We consider the aggregate effects from these and other actions in our next, final chapter.

Additional Principles

Expert and Referent Power
Positive Focus
6 Respectful Disagreement Techniques

For Further Reflection:

1. What do you think are the top biases that affect you (Money, Relationships, Values, Time, Decision-making, Communication)?

2. With what knowledge, skills, and responsibilities are you strong in expert power? Referent power? Where would you like to improve in either of these two areas? What experiences would help you improve?

3. What are some common behavior changes that require positive wordings? (i.e., asking your roommate or apartment mate to "clean up" in a S.M.A.R.T. way versus "not be so messy")

4. Do you offer reasons for your requests?

5. Can you assemble a motivation speech?

6. Do you have a big decision that you are considering? If so, rather than a "Pros & Cons" list, or an "Advantages & Disadvantages" list, you might consider a "What I will gain & What I will lose" list. When students have come to me asking for future career advice, I often ask them about their options, and conclude by asking "5 years from now, which opportunity would you be most upset about if you were not able to pursue it?" This seems to help them prioritize.

7. What would you be willing to debate and defend (which might make some people uncomfortable, as well as make you unpopular with some groups of people)?

8. If you have recently experienced, or witnessed a debate or argument, which rational Scientist tactics did you find most persuasive:

#1. Using principle-centered logic.
#2. Showing the other person's "incomplete logic."
#3. Investigating the other person's causal claims.
#4. Introducing additional evidence.
#5. Using credible analogies.
#6. Being civil, and avoiding "argumentum ad hominem" attacks.

9. Have you ever been offered an apology that was less than sincere? What part of the three-part apology did they do perform most poorly, or forget to do? Did they:

#1. State what they did wrong?
#2. State that they were sorry (or ask for forgiveness)?
#3. Offer to make amends (i.e., if they broke your toy, they offered to replace it)?

For Further Investigation:

Bertram Raven and John French "The bases of social power" *Studies in Social Power*

Gary Yukl, *Leadership in Organizations*

Colin Powell, *My American Journey*

Albert Mehrabian, Morton Weiner, (1967). Decoding of inconsistent communications. *Journal of Personality and Social Psychology*

Albert Mehrabian, Susan Ferris, (1967). Inference of attitudes from nonverbal communication in two channels. *Journal of Consulting Psychology*

David Lapakko, (2007) "Communication is 93% Nonverbal: An Urban Legend Proliferates" Communication and Theatre Association of Minnesota Journal (Vol 34).

Daniel Hamermesh & Jeff Biddle, (1993). "Beauty and the Labor Market," *NBER Working Papers* 4518, National Bureau of Economic Research, Inc.

Jeff Biddle & Daniel Hamermesh, (1998). "Beauty, Productivity and Discrimination: Lawyers' Looks and Lucre," *NBER Working Papers* 5366, National Bureau of Economic Research, Inc.

Gerry Spence, *How to Argue and Win Every Time*

http://www.triallawyerscollege.com/ April 7 09

Ellen Langer, Arthur Blank, and Benzion Chanowitz (1978) "The mindlessness of ostensibly thoughtful action: The role of "placebic" information in interpersonal interaction." *Journal of Personality and Social Psychology* 36, 639-642.

http://www.americanrhetoric.com/speeches/mlkihaveadream.htm April 7 09

http://www.americanrhetoric.com/speeches/billcosbypoundcakespeech.htm April 7 09

Ed Oakly & Dough Krug, *Enlightened Leadership: Getting to the Heart of Change.*

Daniel Kahneman & Amos Tversky, "Prospect Theory: An Analysis of Decision under Risk." *Econometrica*, 1979

http://roomfordebate.blogs.nytimes.com/2009/05/03/ in-the-barracks-out-of-the-closet/

Gary Gates, "Gay men and lesbians in the military: Estimates from Census 2000." The Urban Institute. 2004

Center for Disease Control HIV statistics:
http://www.cdc.gov/hiv/topics/msm/resources/factsheets/msm.htm

http://www.cdc.gov/nchhstp/newsroom/FactSheets.html

Nathaniel Frank, *Unfriendly Fire*, 2009

July 23, 2008, Congressional Statement of Elaine Donnelly, President, Center for Military Readiness, House Armed Services Committee Subcommittee on Personnel, In Support of Section 654 Title 10, the 1993 Law Stating that Homosexuals are not Eligible to Serve in the Military. Rayburn House Office Building, Washington D.C.

The McCormick Freedom Project, "Should the US Military allow openly homosexual members?" DVD Titled "The Struggle Continues: Don't Ask, Don't Tell" http://www.freedomproject.us/

http://whyy.org/cms/radiotimes/2010/02/08/repealing-dont-ask-dont-tell/

http://www.historyplace.com/speeches/clinton-sin.htm

Car loan calculators:
http://www.money-zine.com/Calculators/Auto-Loan-Calculators/Zero-Interest-Car-Loan-Calculator/

http://www.bankrate.com/brm/auto-loan-calculator.asp

The Collective Destinations from Choice

Because they were good individuals, they formed good communities.
Because they were good communities, they formed good nations.
Because they were good nations, they formed a good world.

Once upon a time, in the land of Utopia, there was a large field of grass that was shared by 8 different shepherds, each of whom had 10 sheep. The field, which was approximately 90 square miles in size, was excellent for grazing. Although there were no fences upon the land, the shepherds took their flocks to the same distinct areas each day. These grazing areas were each approximately 10 square miles in size. No flocks grazed upon the middle 10 square miles, as Figure 8-1 shows:

1st Flock	2nd Flock	3rd Flock
4th Flock		5th Flock
6th Flock	7th Flock	8th Flock

Figure 8-1: Common Eating Locations of Grazing Flocks

The sheep of Utopia ate with consistency. One square mile of the field would feed a sheep for a year. As long as each flock stayed in its area, all of the creatures of Utopia lived in harmony. Although the shepherds of the field did not completely understand the balance that had been achieved by the sheep population and its eating behavior (80 sheep used less than 90 square miles of field), everyone was happy.

Unfortunately, during an otherwise uneventful day, one of the shepherds looked at the middle field and thought, "Hmmm, if I were to add one more sheep to my flock, then I could make more money by selling more sheep wool. There looks to be room in the middle section of the field. I think I shall grow my flock by one more sheep."

And so, that shepherd added one more sheep to his flock, and it began to creep into the middle area of the field for grazing. The other shepherds soon observed that one of their fellow community members had added an extra sheep to his flock. Motivated by jealousy, each of the shepherds also added a sheep to their flock. Although the shepherds of the field did not completely understand the balance that had been achieved by the sheep population and its eating behavior (88 sheep used less than 90 square miles of field), everyone was still generally happy, albeit with some slight suspicions of one another.

Unfortunately, during a later, otherwise uneventful day, one of the shepherds looked at the middle field and thought, "Hmmm, there still looks to be room in the middle section of the field. I bet I could add one more sheep to my flock and make more money by selling more sheep wool. I think I shall grow my flock by one more sheep."

Once that additional sheep began grazing upon the middle field, each of the remaining shepherds observed the change and decided to add another sheep to their flocks as well. Although the shepherds of the field did not completely understand the **im**balance that had been achieved by the sheep population and its eating behavior (96 sheep used **more** than 90 square miles of field), everyone was still generally happy—for a little while, anyway.

Eleven months later, it became clear to the shepherds that too many sheep were grazing in the field. Within the next week, before anyone could figure out how many sheep should be sold or who should sell off their sheep, all of the sheep ran out of food and starved to death. The field of Utopia, once lush and green, was now an overgrazed dirt bed and all of its remaining inhabitants were confused and unhappy.

This story of Utopia, based upon Garrett Hardin's *"The Tragedy of the Commons"* speech, offers many insights for *Life* reflection, including:

1. One person's self-interest may become selfish in nature and harmful to others.

2. People cannot always perceive when their actions <u>cause</u> a negative impact (long-term impacts are harder to see), yet bad consequences might still occur.

3. Some mistakes cannot be "corrected" if they occur for too long.

4. People should think intelligently ("accurately predict") about how their (and others') actions will collectively affect their community.

...and while the story of the Utopian field is a fictional tale, consider reading Jared Diamond's non-fiction book, *Collapse: How Societies Choose to Fail or Succeed.* Jared recounts how many societies have failed, including a compelling case about how the inhabitants of Easter Island competed against each other and destroyed all of the trees on the island, which doomed the island's population.

Although ignorant people may not intend their self-centered actions to cause harm, harm they do. As Confucius warned us in the first chapter of this *Life* book, a garden that is not intentionally developed will produce weeds, not fruit. Unfortunately, uncultivated people with self-centered biases not only stifle their own growth, they also reduce the growth of their communities.

The collective consequences from community members' actions greatly affect the types of choices that remain available for individuals. Thus, we will use this final chapter to consider how individual choices combine to affect the destinations available to each person's *Life*.

Strategic *Life* Choices: "To Win," "Not Lose," or "Monkey Win"

This *Life* exploration guide has considered how to analyze, decide and communicate the use of *Money*, *Relationships*, *Time*, and *Values*. With a more cultivated understanding of our individual decisions, we can now focus on three broad strategies that impact community outcomes, whether the community is a partnership, a neighborhood, or a nation. The first two strategies for trying to reach a destination—"Play to Win" and "Play to Not Lose"—each build upon the principle of *risk for reward*. The third strategy of "Monkey Win" will be revealed shortly.

Tennis demonstrates how you can "Play to Win" or "Play to Not Lose." With tennis, you can try to hit the ball so that it simply goes over the net and lands within the boundaries of the other side. This strategy helps you "not lose" points quickly by avoiding major risks with any shot. Alternatively, you can try riskier shots that involve aiming for the opponent's hard-to-reach areas. When successful, this type of risky hitting can quickly lead you to advance in a game. At the same time, these types of shots can be difficult to accomplish, and each unsuccessful attempt negatively affects your chances for winning. Some people always aggressively attempt difficult, winning shots. Others prefer to keep the ball in play and accept the slower, winning pace that accompanies the less risky, "not lose" strategy.

Neither strategy is necessarily ideal in all circumstances, and people will switch between these strategies as they go through *Life*. For example, consider how differently many people view "work risk" before and after they start raising children. Before entering an exclusive relationship, or raising children, people might be more inclined to act like a tennis player who is trying "to win" with every serve and return shot. They go for the big, winning moves. They may boldly fight to be assigned to the most important, visible work projects, as well as have their values and opinions heard during all major decisions. These efforts often involve substantial extra effort (longer work hours, more travel away from home, etc.), and occasionally require confronting another teammate or boss who disagrees with their "big win" plans. If the "big win" people fail while attempting an important project, then their career opportunities may be temporarily stalled or reduced, but that negative outcome will be largely limited to them.

In contrast, after people choose to commit their lives to someone else (such as a romantic partner), or expand their responsibilities to include caring for children, they often transition to a "do not lose" perspective for a period of time. They are more conservative with their actions, and are more interested in "staying in the game." They are less likely to find the extra rewards that accompany a "big win" worth the extra effort, because they prioritize the avoidance of loss more than the seeking of gains. "Do not lose" people have usually obtained good positions in their work lives (earnings, job hours, etc.), and do not wish to risk any type of work demotion.

For people with aggressive personalities, a "do not lose" strategy may appear to be lazy or even cowardly. However, these people should remember the lessons of history. For example, George Washington "defeated" the British, and Scipio "defeated" Hannibal largely by avoiding big risky confrontations, and simply staying in the game while their opponents lost energy and their will to fight. After setting up favorable circumstances for confrontation, Washington and Scipio then switched to "big win" aggressor actions. "Do not lose" can be quite effective as a strategy at the large military group level, or at the individual worker and game player level.

You must cultivate your intelligence to become aware of which strategy makes the most sense for you, even when the tennis analogy does not exactly fit one of your situations. Indeed, you will not always have to win by making someone else lose. Similarly, you also will not always have to compare yourself to others. Play your own game. As George Bernard Shaw has suggested with the following paraphrase:

The reasonable mind adapts to the world,
   The unreasonable mind tries to adapt the world to itself,
      Therefore, all progress depends on unreasonable minds.

Your current position in *Life*, as well as your desired destinations, will strongly influence whether you perceive a situation to be an opportunity or a risk. For example, you are less likely to become an actor or an actress if you do not go to an audition, yet each audition also requires risking (temporary) failure and disappointment. Similarly, certain schools also have a prestigious reputation because they are difficult, but if you survive their rigorous programs and graduate from them, you will benefit from the job placement and networking opportunities that accompany that prestige.

Over time, you may even begin to see a pattern of the "big win" aggressors often being people who either have "nothing to lose" or people who have already accumulated enough wins that they can afford some losses if their riskier endeavors do not pay off (because their rewards from risky efforts that did succeed were often greater than the losses from the efforts that did not succeed). The "do not lose" personalities have typically grown to a point where they do not wish to risk any major losses or setbacks. As their circumstances change (e.g., house mortgage is paid off, children's college funds established), these people may become more aggressive with the development of their *Life* controls.

Although we each have unique "win" destinations, we also share common "loss" destinations. As we shall soon see, our individual losses can add up to become significant losses for our communities and our nation. Consider the control of our money. Perhaps the biggest "loss" possibility that graduates will encounter occurs when they first leave school. If people buy the most expensive car that they can afford "on credit," and then buy or rent the most expensive housing that they can afford, then these individuals obligate themselves to producing a certain amount of money each year. These people will have little chance to grow or explore new options because they must pay off what they have acquired. Purchasing too many things too soon often obligates people to constantly work. Their chances for rest, reflection, and relaxation decrease as their debt increases. Degrading to a status of "maximum effort just to maintain a standard of living" is a "loss" in the win-loss column of one's *Life*.

Contrast this materialistic approach with intelligent graduates who find affordable, and reliable, transportation options (maybe even biking or public transportation) and simple (versus elaborate) housing for their first few years after school. They quickly develop savings that can be used for investing. Wise financial advisors do NOT suggest that you "spend only what you earn," or "live within your means." Instead, they suggest that you spend "well below your earnings" and have a large investment focus while you are young (because as you grow older, you will probably become married, raise children, and need more money).

This "spend below" advice is not about dampening your spending desires—it is about preserving your future freedom just in case you want to leave a future job (lousy boss, lousy work schedule, lousy pay, etc.). When you have no savings, your ability to negotiate and choose in *Life* is greatly limited. Wealthy leverage helps. By living well below your means, you are able to feel tremendous freedom, versus constantly worry about bill collectors. Not investing, even just a little money in a low-risk investment every month, is a "loss." As a colleague of mine stated, "If you live for years and spend less than you make, then you shall always have money."

As a national community, one of America's recognized money weaknesses is its government's national debt—it spends more than it collects. Similarly, as individuals, American citizens save relatively little. If each individual lived within a budget that included saving, more investment dollars would be available as loans for our productive citizens and businesses. The nation would be more prosperous. A far less prosperous outcome awaits America if it does not change its money behaviors. One of America's main expense programs—the Social Security system—is projected to go bankrupt by 2050. The collective money behaviors of America need to change, or some degrading collapses within our society will occur.

Not all spending behaviors are "losses" that lead to collapse. For example, accepting a short-term car loan, or buying professional work clothes with a credit card, or using school loans, can actually be growth investments. If you must go into debt and borrow against the future, it should probably be to enhance your ability to perform your core competencies, or expand your skills and abilities. Big expenditures should support your growth.

Even little, daily decisions can lead to large differences in your wealth. As Ben Franklin once advised, "Watch the pennies and the dollars will take care of themselves." There can be an enormous dollar difference between going out for dinner and a movie with someone versus making dinner together at home, buying some snacks at a grocery store, and renting a movie. Sometimes, a night-away of "escaping" is worth the expense. At other times, the stay-at-home approach is preferred. Making such choices with awareness, and not merely because of habit, reflects people's intelligent analysis of their positions in *Life*.

After analyzing their goals for a while, many people conclude that money should not be their number one priority, at least not for lasting fulfillment. Although Americans are some of the richest inhabitants on the planet, we are not (on average) the happiest. It takes outcomes other than money to make us happy. Indeed, some of the self-cultivated, W.C.M.J. sages from the *Values* chapter who taught about self-development were not materially rich (i.e., Jesus Christ led a simple life, yet His teachings remain the most widely read on the planet).

More generally, people usually do not want money for money's sake. People want money for what they can do with it. Whether people use money's purchasing power for advancing their relationships, intelligence, or time (via a time-savings device), money is simply an aid for reaching a larger goal. Creating, sorting, and prioritizing among those goals has been one of the main explorations of this *Life* book. Proper cultivation and pursuit of these goals can lead to the "eudemonia" fulfillment that so many of the great minds have sought.

Unfortunately, people can become distracted from this long-term fulfillment quest by the almost limitless, short-term wants that bombard their every day existence. These "wants" answer the question "How much is enough?" with the response "Just a little more."

Short-term wants can lead to "loss." An African priest once told me about a clever way in which African trappers catch monkeys. The trappers begin by slicing a coconut into two halves. The trappers then hollow out the coconut halves, and cut a hole in one of the halves that is barely big enough to allow a monkey's hand to pass through it. Before reconnecting the two coconut halves, a sweet smelling orange is placed inside of the hollow shell. The coconut halves are then rejoined using rope. Lastly, the "coconut surprise" is fastened to a tree. The trappers leave.

Eventually, a monkey will travel by the area and, upon smelling the scent of the orange, find the coconut that contains the orange. The monkey then slides its hand through the hole and grabs the orange. When the monkey attempts to pull out its hand while holding the orange, its hand is too big to exit the coconut. The determined monkey, so fixated on that orange, continues to hang on to that orange and pull, all the while remaining stuck within the coconut. Maybe the monkey sees the oncoming trappers, maybe it does not. Either way, the trappers simply stroll in and place a cage around the monkey and the coconut. The monkey's poor choice results in its capture.

It makes you wonder what that monkey was thinking during it final moments of freedom.

"I see trappers coming, should I let go of this orange?"

"NO! It can satisfy my short-term desires! Oh, how I want it so!"

"Maybe it will come out with this tug, before those trappers catch me!"

"Drat."

Monkey-ing around with Relationships

Your choice to remain single, or to add a partner to your *Life* travels, is quite likely THE LARGEST EARTHLY INFLUENCE UPON YOUR HAPPINESS DURING YOUR LIFE. With a supportive partner, you will fight any Goliath-like challenge. With a draining partner, you will be fortunate to make it through a day without anguish. Oddly, as obvious as the advice "choose a good partner" is, desires such as F.L.Y.—A.S.I.A. can make people look as primitive as monkeys. Many people do not like to feel alone, and they become more susceptible to their ever present F.L.Y.—A.S.I.A. wants. Fortunately, we can cultivate ourselves to intelligently think above the raw desires of a "gold digger" or a "cradle robber," as well as ask better questions than the stereotypical "What does he do?" and "What does she look like?" We can and must cultivate beyond our monkey urges. As one South African mother of three daughters said to me after she learned that I was a father with a daughter, "You be sure to tell your daughter that 'Before a young man is 25, any female to him is just an experiment.'" This advice, while a bit extreme in tone, remains insightful for many 18-25 year-olds.

Short-term wants can lead people to a short-term "monkey win," and its accompanying long-term "loss." Much like the monkey, some humans simply cannot accurately predict the future, long-term consequences from their short-term desires. They have not cultivated the intellectual or spiritual portion of their P.I.E.S. hierarchy. How many times have you learned about how the "monkey win" temptations of sex have ruined somebody's life? How many affairs by politicians, athletes, Hollywood celebrities, and spiritual leaders have shown how the supposedly simple act of procreation can dominate people's thought processes so much that they experience a "loss" of career status and reputation? This historical struggle of people trying to master their "monkey win" urges from their sex drive was well stated by Augustine of Hippo over 1,600 years ago when he wrote, "Oh God, grant me celibacy…but not just yet!"

A great beginning "do not lose" strategy for relationships is to focus on being a good single person. Anyone can be single, but how many people perform being single well? How many people dare to be a little different and devote time to grow something meaningful about themselves (a talent, a charity, a core competency, etc.)? How many graduates are willing to spend one night per week (or more?), or one afternoon each weekend doing some growth activity that will also make them a more interesting person?

Consider how living like a single person can be like playing a piano. Anyone can play a piano—at its most basic level, a pianist places her fingers on piano keys and presses down. However, not many people cultivate their skills enough—through deliberate practice—to sell over a million albums of their music (or singing), as Josh Groban has. Those who do not cultivate their skills to a higher level will not earn the opportunity of a concert crowd.

Similarly, those singles that do not live their lives well, with an awareness toward growth, stand a good chance of becoming bored with their lives, and succumbing to a F.L.Y.—A.S.I.A. urge. These uncultivated people will probably fill their existence with the obvious, although not best, option of another person who is also interested in "monkey win" sex. Each person may not even value their sex partner—only the sex. So, when you are single, remember to enjoy other people's company, without pressuring yourself to achieve a "monkey win" of sexual relations. As research has shown, better relationship success comes from people who use their cultivated neo-cortex to match up with other cultivated people who know what they stand for and for what they will fight (such as common religious beliefs). For more insights about relationships, consider reading Gary Becker's *A Treatise on the Family* or John Gottman's *Why Marriages Succeed or Fail*.

Before risking an over-commitment "loss" to the wrong type of person, people might consider asking the following question that a mythical man named "Jack" once asked. Once upon a time, Jack was on an "enjoy and explore" date with Jill (Jack was interested in Jill, but not yet head-over-heels committed to asking her to be his exclusive partner). Jack asked Jill if she was better at starting relationships or maintaining them. Jill replied "Starting, most of my relationships have not lasted." Over the course of a few more dates, Jack tried to uncover if Jill could intelligently explain (a.k.a., "predict") what kind of a partner she thought would be good for her. After all, Jack was committing valuable time to Jill that he could have been investing in someone else. Jack also waited to hear how Jill had changed her approach to dating, or how she was better at determining who would be most compatible with her. Alas, no such growth actions were spoken. Jill said that she did not want to think that hard about "love"—it was just a "feeling." Such discussions were a priority to Jack, but not to Jill. They parted on good terms.

The "start or maintain a relationship" question can be useful because some people work very hard in the beginning of their relationships and then, once an exclusive relationship has been established, quit building and growing the relationship. Instead, they downshift and contribute only some lower level of "maintenance" energy. For some reason, these people believe that they no longer need to develop their relationship and that it will somehow grow by itself. Without the continued investment by both partners, relationship growth will be hard to achieve. A collective "loss" occurs for both members if they do not pursue growth in their relationship.

Sadly, some people make money by promoting lesser cultivated, monkey relationship behaviors, which can cause collective collapses within a community. Consider some of the songs that musicians sell. I once heard a song on my radio with lyrics (from females, no less) that were something along the lines of:

"If I, want to take a guy, home with me tonight,
    It's none of your business,
        And if she, wants to be a freak and, sell it on the weekend,
            It's none of your business."

Really? The facts suggest otherwise, as James Wilson has compiled in his book *The Marriage Problem*. For example, James discusses research by William Galston, which has demonstrated that you only need to do three things in order to avoid living in poverty in America:

1. Finish high school.
2. Marry before having a child.
3. Produce children after the age of 20.

William's research includes the fact that 79 percent of the people that he studied who did not prioritize and achieve all three of these outcomes ended up in poverty—a definite "loss."

Beyond William's research, yet still related, is the consistent trend that out-of-wedlock births often result in the child being raised by a single parent. These children with a single parent have a greater likelihood of committing a crime (raising a child and cultivating her or his value system is demanding enough for two parents—and even more difficult for a single parent!). Thus, in response to the people who believe that moral judgments about sexual activity are "none of your business," an intelligent person may respond, "If you understood causality, you would not sing that."

For non-cultivated individuals, these types of self-gratifying, "monkey win" songs are appealing, and possibly even validating. Ignorant people will want to believe in the "advice" of these songs. Unlike "stupid" people, who know the difference between "right" and "wrong" and still choose the wrong option, "ignorant" people genuinely do not know any better. They may be vulnerable to "monkey win," primitive persuasion. Lacking any higher intelligence about sex drives, ignorant people follow their raw feelings, and feel justified telling other people that it is "None of your business." In reality, the higher taxes that community members pay to support other people's welfare, or pay to prevent crimes from deviant children, or pay for prison facilities, makes it clear that immature, uncultivated people are everybody's business. Just as it only takes a few ignorant people carelessly dropping their trash to ruin the beauty of a landscape, it only takes a few misguided thoughts to ruin a person's winning ways, and create a "loss" of valuable money, relationships, time, and values for themselves and fellow community members.

With regard to the *Life* control of time, some people achieve a short-term "monkey win" and a long-term "loss" because of their health choices. The long-term consequences of these choices are not immediately obvious. For example, some twenty-year olds will wake up at 7 a.m. in the morning, drink a caffeinated beverage and maybe even use a tobacco product to "kick start" their bodies into action. Alternatively, other twenty year-olds awaken at 6 a.m. and begin jogging, swimming, weightlifting, yoga-ing, or some other type of fitness growth. By 8 a.m., both types of people are on their way to work. At age 21, their overall health differences may not appear to be that different. However, by age 30, their one-hour morning difference in habits will have created some different physical outcomes. Can you predict some of those likely differences?

Those differences have consequences. Consider the second, big national money fear that sometime around the year 2050 the United States government will become bankrupt due to its other major expense— government supported health care costs (Medicare, Medicaid, etc.). Imagine how those costs would decrease if people would cultivate themselves to reduce their short-term monkey gratifications from sugar, salt, and fat, and instead live a healthier strategy of "eat a little less, and move a little more." The savings from such preventative, versus artificially restorative, health efforts would be immense! An easy "Win" for a cultivated graduate to see, but tougher for the monkey-minded. For an extreme example of the effects of poor eating habits, consider watching the movie *Super Size Me*.

Cultivating an ability to understand long-term consequences from short-term actions can be difficult. Watching too much television, or too many movies, can slowly condition some people to expect that many of *Life's* major decisions can be understood and solved beautifully in two hours or less. This "time frame bias" and "Hollywood Beauty" bias can lead people to become impatient and distracted with the slower, grittier progression of real time. Some people do not wish to devote any effort toward developing a deeper understanding of *Life's* time. In contrast, you can expand your understanding and control of time by reading a book such as Deepak Chopra's *Ageless Body, Timeless Mind.*

Besides making you more healthy, prioritizing what you value throughout time can even save your life, as evidenced in Victor Frankl's book *Man's Search for Meaning.* Victor recounts his survival of Auschwitz and other World War II concentration camps, and how his deep investigation into what was worthy of his efforts helped him stay alive and survive the darkest of pains. Victor's story speaks to the need to cultivate our neo-cortex abilities.

Long before Victor's insights, Confucius spoke about people's struggle to cultivate themselves, as well as the challenge to overcome short-term, ego-gratifying "monkey wins." For example, he said:

"The fact remains that I have never seen a man who loved virtue as much as sex."

"Demand much from yourself, little from others, and you will prevent discontent."

"A gentleman resents his incompetence; he does not resent his obscurity."

For an expanded exploration of this concept, consider performing the following experiment: Make a list of some of the "great thinkers" who have changed a community, a nation, or the world. Next, study a few of their lives, via books, documentaries, etc. As you study, consider how many of their value systems were associated with "monkey priorities" such as "My life was fulfilling because I sought out multiple sex partners." More than likely, you will find that a large part of their rewarding lives came from cultivating their *Life* and using it to solve seemingly impossible problems (e.g., violent wars, racism, poverty). Although they would have encountered many "monkey win" distractions, they were cultivated enough to pursue growth goals, and happier as a result.

This effort to cultivate and advance ourselves occurs as a battle of wills, often within ourselves and on a nearly daily basis. It might even start with the alarm clock and the Jekyll & Hyde discussions that occur in your head.

"Get up."

"No."

"You need to exercise."

"No, I need to sleep."

"Snooze for 10 more minutes, and then go for a morning walk?"

"Snooze for 20, and then hit the gym on the way home from work…audio book while travelling."

…and similar, inner discussions of priorities occur throughout the day.

During those morning inner discussions, how do you value your upcoming day? Do you begin by thinking of the years of effort that it took for you to reach your current *Life* position? This "living from the past" perspective can sometimes be draining. Consider an alternative way of perceiving each day. Consider starting with, "Look at what an interesting position I have achieved…how should I grow from here?" For example, by the time I finished writing chapter six of this book, my mind began to think, "That took a lot of effort." Then one day, as I was reflecting on the *sunk cost bias*, I started thinking, "Today I start the day with the goal of writing an eight-chapter book, and six chapters have already been written. I am nearly finished, and will be even further along by the end of this week." This positively affected my perspective and increased my motivation to complete my research.

Similar, positive growth cultivation can occur during your travel time to school or work. Certainly, there are times when clearing your head with silence, or escaping with music for a while, helps recharge you. At the same time, there are probably also some opportunities when you can listen to a "book on CD" from a local library, or some interesting download from *iTunes U*, or an intelligent talk-radio program. Alternatively, you could use your travel time (if you are not driving) to apply the 3 Wise Questions (or 5? Or 7?) to the questions within this book (and beyond) that cultivate a deeper understanding of who you are and who you wish to be.

Your ability to consistently focus effort, versus surrendering to the forces of entropy, is a challenge that not everyone has understood or mastered. As Thomas Kempis once wrote, "Fight like a (hu)man! Habit is overcome by habit…" Similarly, Aristotle stated that we are what we repeatedly do; excellence is not an act, but a habit. For a comparison of the different habits that younger people develop, consider seeing the film *2 Million Minutes*, which contrasts the daily decisions of high school students in the United States, India, and China. Your *Life* habits guide you toward your destinations, little by little, day by day. *Life* is now. *Life* happens with daily decisions. Be more than a monkey.

This type of self-cultivation does not require millions of dollars, but it can lead you to million dollar ideas and jobs, and priceless internal satisfaction. For example, general intelligence—sometimes called *specific g*—has been shown to be one of the best, if not the best, predictor of work performance, as research by Malcolm Ree and his colleagues has shown. Equipping your mind with a variety of mental tools allows it to draw upon lessons learned and choose the most effective actions. A second major success factor is the ability to tackle challenges with an effort of *conscientiousness* that reflects excellence, consistency, and intention. For more insights into these factors, consider reading a study on personality and outcomes, such as the one by Murray Barrick and Michael Mount listed at the end of this chapter.

A cultivated, growth-oriented mindset is not only good for you, it may also make your communication more persuasive. Once, while studying at RAND, I had the good fortune of joining fellow students at a lunch table with Michael, a member of RAND's student selection committee. Michael had to decide who would be offered one of the limited number of RAND student slots. Michael had reviewed all of our applications, as well as those applications that did not result in an invitation to study at RAND. Michael shared with us a communication factor that really stood out among our application essays. He said that we had not simply stated that we were "looking forward to learning" (a self-interest that could be perceived as selfish), but that we were also looking forward to doing something with the knowledge that we would gain. We had articulated credible future goals that we believed would help grow our communities and nations as a result of our education. Such a cultivated level of interest reflected the world-impacting effects that RAND sought from its students.

I have tried to pass this valuable piece of insight on to my students whenever they apply for a job or an advanced school—it is not enough to say "I am happy to be considered," or "I look forward to learning." Instead, you should display your expert and referent power by learning about that school or job position, and then authentically tell a story about what you will do and grow with that opportunity if you are selected.

Cultivating yourself can also occur by acting with a "How can I help" attitude. It takes so little effort to go from an attitude of "it's all about me" to "I will help," yet what a difference it can make. Have you ever had a lousy experience with a waitress or waiter? Even though you visit a restaurant primarily for its food, poor service can dramatically lower the experience. Good service can also greatly improve the experience. The waiter who approaches the job with an attitude of "How can I help make the customer's experience great?" will usually earn a much higher tip than the one who approaches the work with an attitude of "How many more drinks do I have to drop off at that table before I can go home?"

Graduates will most likely find that the deliberate practice of acting in a helpful way will improve their ability to perform with excellence, consistency, and intention. Those who authentically earn a helpful reputation will eventually have others bragging about them and recommending them to other community members (e.g., potential employers, dating networks, eBay customers). The effect from using an attitude (good or bad) is similar to the effect of a pebble dropped in a pond of water—it expands in ripples, makes contact with others, and ultimately returns (to you). Research about the outcomes from helpful and selfish value systems has been performed via computer tournaments. To gain insights from some of the results, consider reading Robert Axelrod's *The Evolution of Cooperation*. His book will expand your intelligence about the benefits of being nice, provoke-able, and forgiving.

At a larger, community level, consider how "helping others" is actually a type of "enlightened self-interest" suggested by Alexis de Tocqueville nearly 200 years ago in his book *Democracy in America*. For example, when a business tries to create a better MP3 player by combining it with a cell phone and an internet browser, it does so because it believes that the helpful features will appeal to customers. A "helping others" perspective can be beneficial to a business, government agency, charity, or any community organization trying to achieve goals.

Even with helpful efforts, no one will be perfect all of the time. Fortunately, since we have all made mistakes, most of us are willing to forgive mistakes by others. Remember to consider the intent of someone's efforts, and not only the result. For example, suppose that a loved one wants to help you start your day by bringing you breakfast in bed. What if they accidentally burn the last pieces of bread available for toast? When they arrive at your bed, they may have an embarrassed look on their face. Would you get upset at this breakfast of juice and burnt bread? Of course not. Although the breakfast results may not be optimal, the effort of making you breakfast would be greatly appreciated.

At the same time, evaluating intentions and performance becomes more difficult as the importance of the outcomes increase, such as within work and romantic relationships. There are times when we expect results from others. If people constantly break their promises to help us, or brag without achieving results, then their results force us to be suspicious about whether they should be trusted in the future.

There will also be times when we will evaluate our own intentions, efforts, and results, such as when we review our prioritization lists from Chapter 1. When these reflections start, remember that you have an average life expectancy of around 80 years (probably longer if you are already cultivated enough to choose reasonable food and fitness options). When you make an error, it helps to think about how that error fits into your long-term journey and destination. Avoid focusing exclusively on the immediate consequences of that bad choice (e.g., bad job, wrong educational choice, wrong romance). Instead, consider including in your reflections a longer time period of your performance. For example, do not ask yourself, "Am I better this hour than I was last hour?" Instead, ask yourself "Am I better at _____ (fill in the blank) now than I was last year?" or perhaps "Have I grown in _____ (fill in the blank) since last month?" Similarly, if you were to examine your understanding and use of your *Money, Relationships, Time* and *Values* controls at each birthday of your life, would you see an overall trend of growth?

If you should happen to uncover some poor choices within your prior journeys, remember that today is a new day. The *sunk cost bias* still applies. As the philosopher John Dewey has suggested, perfection does not have to be a person's final goal. Looking forward in time, the good person is the person who, no matter how bad they acted yesterday, starts acting with more goodness today. The bad person is the person who, no matter how good they acted yesterday, starts acting worse today. Now is the time to use your effort and ability to grow toward a goal, or series of goals. Now. A sunk cost cliché with truth: Today is the beginning of the rest of your *Life*.

These steps toward cultivation are like hiking to reach a treasure placed at the top of a mountain—the reward is not visible until you have already used a good deal of energy to travel part of the way. This type of "work" takes faith to attempt. While numerous people have written about the reward, the reward is not initially obvious—especially to monkey minds. You have to be a "*Life* Climber" to understand it. Once you do understand it, your motivation for the quest will likely increase. During that climb to the top, remember that much of the life of the mountain occurs before the top— be sure to enjoy the journey.

Growing the "United" Community

Our intelligence—our ability to accurately predict—reflects of our understanding of causality over time. Those graduates who are able to realistically imagine how future destinations can be reached as a result of their prior choices are the graduates who are most likely to achieve happiness, versus disappointment, from their decisions. Cultivated intelligence, at the individual and collective level, is rather fragile. Consider this thought experiment:

Imagine a large cage with five monkeys in it. Near the center of the cage is a stack of boxes with a bunch of bananas placed at the top. Question: How would you stop a cage full of monkeys from trying to eat the bananas?

A possible answer follows (this is only a thought experiment...do not try this at home):

After the monkeys have been placed in the cage, position a fire hose outside of the cage, ready to unleash a painful spray of water. The moment that one of the monkeys starts to climb the boxes toward the bananas, spray all five monkeys. After a few attempts, the five monkeys will understand not to go near those boxes. Now, remove one monkey and bring in a brand new monkey. Inevitably, the new monkey will want to follow its natural instincts and climb up those boxes toward the bananas. As soon as the new monkey tries to move toward the boxes, spray all of the monkeys with the rushing water. This will make the original four monkeys mad and they will likely start to physically punish the curious, climbing monkey.

Next, take out another of the original monkeys and add in a new resident monkey. The other monkeys, having been conditioned by their previous experiences, will now likely use discouraging physical force on the new monkey whenever they perceive it moving toward those bananas.

If you continue the pattern of changing out the oldest resident monkey one at a time, three more times, eventually you will be left with a cage full of monkeys that will attack any new monkey that moves toward the boxes. A new mindset will control the community, even if none of the members remember why they no longer pursue their original banana inclinations.

The previous thought experiment suggests that each new generation of community members (even simple ones made of monkeys) can be cultivated, or degenerated, toward habits, perspectives, and rules that differ from their original behaviors. These generational time changes can impact an entire community. For example, the United States has experienced this phenomenon and collectively changed its behaviors multiple times. As evidence of one such change, consider examining the United States Declaration of Independence. You will notice that it begins with "...of the thirteen united States of America." The word "States" is capitalized, while the word "united" is not. This state-centric attitude of the revolutionaries dominated the thinking of the 1770s. Their "states first" attitude continued after the colonies defeated the British Empire and gained independence, as documented in the Articles of Confederation.

However, it soon became apparent that the Articles were not producing a very effective governmental system. This led to another gathering of state representatives. This time, the members who met were not merely individuals from states that disliked British rule. The members had cultivated a new mindset, similar to being a new generation of individuals. This time, they were "brothers in arms" who had risked their lives and lands together in earlier battles. They were "United" in their cause to form a United States with a significant federal government. After creating and agreeing upon a new Constitution, the United States began to be mentioned as a singular entity (The United States "is") versus as a group of individual states (the united States "are"). A similar, generational unity appeared after World War II when America and its allies defeated the Nazis and their partners.

Question: Have the original founding ideas of the greatest nation and grandest experiment in self-government been eroded? Lacking an international threat to our country's viability, have we begun to degenerate from within? While robust evidence and answers to that question would require a separate book, a cursory look at some of America's founding ideals vis-à-vis one of its current behaviors seems worthwhile.

Let us briefly begin looking at America's founding ideals via its Declaration of Independence. One of the Declaration's statements affirmed that there were certain "unalienable rights" for Americans. These rights were foundational to how American people were to be governed. These rights came from the people's "Creator," also mentioned as "Nature's God" as well as the "Supreme Judge of the world." Three of these rights were "Life, Liberty and the pursuit of Happiness." America was different. America's European explorers were entrepreneurs funded by royal courts and companies that were willing accept risks in pursuit of rewards. These business ventures helped establish an American mindset of working hard to achieve a reward.

America continued to grow in this mindset from generations of individuals who left oppressive governments and faced life-threatening boat rides from Europe so that they could begin new lives. The "risk for reward" culture also continued to be strengthened in the 1800s as Americans moved west and explored the unknown frontiers. These efforts reinforced a belief that Americans were allowed to be physically and socially mobile. Americans are still less concerned with where people come from (e.g., aristocratic class, a particular religion, or a particular ethnicity). Instead, they are more concerned about where people are going. An American ethic of independence, hard work, and a desire for limited government interference can be seen throughout America's beginnings, as well as its growth.

This ethic of individual responsibility was accompanied by another American trait during the Colonial period—virtue. As one of America's Founding Fathers, and its second President of the United States, John Adams said, "Our Constitution was made only for a moral and religious people. It is wholly inadequate to the government of any other." The cultivated virtue of Americans was one of the reasons that the early leadership of the United States could write such a minimally-worded Constitution, which remains the longest active-working Constitution in the world. America's culture and governmental foundation, based upon Founders who had studied over 2,000 years of histories, was uniquely different from the rest of the world. However, because of its unique values and behaviors, this foundation was strong.

Unfortunately, at least one currently legal behavior suggests that, over time, certain people have monkey-ed with, and degraded, America's unalienable rights. More specifically, abortion-for-convenience goes counter to the declared value and self-evident truth that Americans have a right to "Life." The current abortion-for-convenience role modeling of our nation indirectly advocates for other nation's abortion-for-convenience policies, some of which are performed with significant discrimination. For example, some parts of the world perform over 90% of their abortions on defenseless girls, because they are perceived to be an economic drain on that culture's families (due to dowries, etc.). Whether it is for social convenience or career convenience, uncultivated, condition-free abortions nudge a society toward the F.L.Y.—A.S.I.A. selfishness of a "monkey win community," instead of a cultivated, *Life*-growing, humane society. This suggests that some people who are less than "moral and religious" have influenced American culture, politics, and behaviors.

America's laws with regard to Liberty have traditionally attempted to balance benefits to society with constraining individual behaviors (e.g., speed limits, legal drinking age). These laws have been based upon probable outcomes, and as our American community has become more intelligent, American policies have changed to ensure that individual liberty does not negatively impact other community members. For example, during the last 20 years, as science has informed our nation of the life dangers associated with tobacco smoke, our society has begun restricting the locations and circumstances under which people can smoke.

During that same time period, science has also revealed that from the moment of conception, a microscopic human possesses all of the information necessary to grow through all forms of human life, including "zygote," "infant," "adult," and "senior citizen." For some reason, abortion has not been restricted accordingly. Why? The answers appear to be political and emotional in nature, but not rational. As a result, abortion-for-convenience has violated the unalienable right to community-considered Liberty as well as "the pursuit of Happiness." If you choose to further cultivate yourself with these issues, consider studying topics such as "Natural Law Philosophy" and "Civil Liberties." Audio-CD teachings, such as Joseph Koterski's *Natural Law and Human Nature* and John Finn's *Civil Liberties and the Bill of Rights,* are available at www.teach12.com.

For those Americans that are fortunate enough to be born within America's citizenry, or acquire citizenship later in their *Life*, they are not guaranteed anything, but they are entitled to a "pursuit." As anyone who has ever played competitive sports knows, not everyone wins all of the time. The pursuit of happiness is often accompanied with failure and disappointment, as ESPN's Greatest Athlete of the Century, Michael Jordan, has noted in his "Failure" commercial for Nike, which may be viewed on YouTube.

Throughout American history, people worked hard and risked failure in part because there was often a financial incentive associated with the successful achievement of their goals. Today, American capitalism still offers competition and rewards for those who seek to develop ideas and sell products. Although not everyone will be the top winner, many people benefit from the jobs and products that are produced by the winners. Some of this competitive growth includes "creative destruction" that results in technology replacing humans. Consider the technology of bank ATMs. Many bank tellers lost their jobs when ATMs were created. However, customers gained significant convenience because ATMs provided people with 24-hour access to their bank accounts. Everyone benefited from this convenience, even those who did not use the ATMs, because the lines inside of the banks became shorter. Additionally, banking fees decreased because one 24-hour machine cost less than multiple bank tellers. Over the long-term, a new industry of ATM technology was formed, and people gained the opportunity to work in new ATM production, sales, and maintenance jobs.

However, while society benefited, there was a short-term loss for bank tellers (who could still pursue employment elsewhere). If there had been a strong Bank Teller's Union (BTU), perhaps there would have been heated BTU strikes and picketing against the implementation of ATMs. The BTU would have emphasized the job losses, knowing that "loss messages" can affect an audience more than "gain messages" by almost a two-to-one impact. However, with hindsight, we can see that ATMs were the greater benefit to society, in the same way that society benefited when the telegraph replaced the Pony Express, or when cars replaced horse and buggy transportation. Creative destruction is a form of growth that allows more beneficial goods and services to emerge.

Some monkey minds want to demonize capitalistic systems. They claim that capitalism turns an individual's self-interest into a selfish greed that victimizes others. This causal claim ignores the numerous examples of selfish behavior, corruption, and greed found in other systems of government, including the socialist and communist varieties. The opportunity for self-interest to turn into "greed" is present in all communities and individuals. Rather than blaming capitalism's "creative destruction" for somebody's "victimization," these monkey minds should look at how non-winning persons are using their *Life* controls—clues may exist that the "victims" have made poor choices.

When wrong choices are made, whether at the individual, business, or governmental level, the results may include the suffering of negative consequences. Suffering, whether at an individual or national level is a clue (and not always a gentle one). This clue informs the individual or community that it is out of harmony with some combination of *Life* controls and destinations. For those individuals and communities that are suffering, a principled-question should be asked: Have they stopped growing their skills and talents (e.g., physically, emotionally, intellectually, spiritually)?

Whether sports teams, businesses, or nations, communities that perform at productive levels should be studied to see how their methods might be adopted by others seeking productive growth. The American system of risk, reward, and loss has produced unrivaled research, development, and innovation. The fruits from this cultivated capitalism can be seen in a range of outcomes, from business sector iPhones to government adventures in moon landings. It can also be seen in "the Berlin Wall experiment." Following World War II, Berlin was divided and its residents were subjected to two different kinds of government systems. The capitalistic system produced a noticeably better standard of living for the residents. Since World War II, America's core competency of capitalism, and the productivity that accompanies it, has been measured through national level data such as Gross Domestic Product (GDP), number of patents, and number of Nobel Laureates. Rather than delving into further statistics, two questions may be asked that will directly allow people to reflect on America's productive growth:

1.   Would you rather live as an upper class money earner in America in 1950, or a middle class earner in American in the present? (Hint: Consider no cell phones or computers...)

2.   Would you rather live in the United States, or somewhere else?

Your answers will likely suggest that the U.S. system should be emulated, not degenerated. This level of respect for the United States goes beyond our own citizenry. While serving a military rotation in Afghanistan, I enjoyed the camaraderie of my translators, who were natives of Afghanistan. Many chose to work hard and then come to America because it is still known as "The Land of Opportunity."

The United States offers a very unique environment for the growth and pursuit of happiness. Not everyone wants to work 70 or more hours per week in pursuit of wealth. That is a reasonable choice. Oddly, some non-70ers become jealous of the wealth that many 70ers acquire (e.g., Bill Gates, Steve Jobs, Andrew Carnegie, John Rockefeller). Odder still, some non-70ers get jealous and start to politically push for laws that take away from the rewards that the 70ers have earned. This reduces the motivation of individuals who might otherwise try to be a 70er. At a community and national level, these "take from others' success" policies lead to less motivation and innovation, which leads to fewer jobs for non-70ers.

You would not raise a child or a sports team to ignore the fact that a lack of performance will reduce your rewards. Unfortunately, we occasionally forget this basic rule of growth. Occasionally, well-intentioned government policy makers create overly-generous benefits for people who have not shown the evidence for performing productively with their *Life* controls. For example, beginning around the year 2002, well-intentioned government policies set the interest rates for home loans at very low levels. The gesture helped make home loans more available to more Americans—even those who could not really afford them.

A plague of overly-generous loans were then offered to people who, if they had developed a basic budget like those in the *Time* chapter, should have known that they could not have afforded their loans. At the same time, if banks had used better lending standards, then they would not have offered so many loans to so many high risk applicants. The resulting housing mortgage market collapse could have predicted. See John Taylor's *Getting Off Track : What Prolonged the Crisis* for more insights. There is a compelling case that overly generous rewards (improbably low interest rates, easy qualifications, etc.) accelerated a housing boom and then an incredible banking bust, leading to a tightening of credit markets, lower business activity, fewer jobs, and higher unemployment. John's book points out a compelling link in this causal chain.

More generally, when government policies create "safety nets" that are too large, some people stop analyzing their decisions with their *Life* controls of *Money, Relationships, Time,* and *Values.* They exert less effort than if they were taking risks with their own controls. This entropy degrades collective effort. Too much "safety," without penalties for non-performance, leads some people to become either lazy or reckless. This can harm the individual's community. Even the well-intentioned attempts by Franklin Roosevelt caused damage by rewarding underperformers and reducing achievement incentives. Compelling evidence of Roosevelt's negative impacts can be found in Burton Folsom Jr.'s book, *New Deal or Raw Deal?*

If we want to create a community that offers opportunity for everyone, then we should create laws that reward people for achieving their goals without simultaneously creating laws that harm people's chances to grow. Similarly, if people do not achieve success, especially if they chose not to work hard to advance themselves, then they should be made aware of the consequences of their choices. They should be cultivated to learn from their mistakes. Even though it may be politically popular to give hand outs to under-performers by taking from the success achieved by others, these collective policies stifle America's growth.

Francis Bacon once warned that we must use the right methods to reach our conclusions (and destinations). Otherwise, when people (even geniuses) use the wrong methods they arrive at the wrong conclusion—or in the case of geniuses, they arrive at the wrong conclusions faster. America has benefited from great citizens who have used the right methods to lead America down productive paths and toward positive futures. To acquaint yourself with some of America's cultivated, growth-oriented leaders and paths, consider reading William Bennett's series, *America, the Last, Best Hope. "Scientia potentia est…"*

Lastly, as a useful mental exercise on what happens when a government starts rewarding under-performers, consider the massive book, or an audiobook edition, of Ayn Rand's *Atlas Shrugged.* She presents a thought experiment on the degradation of the American spirit of competition, and the resulting national entropy and world collapse. For anyone who would dare to succeed, this book (or audio-CD set) is essential, and enjoyable, cultivation.

*****

The Vessel of You

You are a vessel with two possible forms. The first form is like a cup, or a receiving glass. Your vessel, or state of "Being," has been filled by many different influences, such as parents, friends, teachers, and employers. One way to examine the influence of others on your cup of Being is to answer the questions at the end of each chapter—after your initial answers, use The Wise Questions to uncover why you responded with such answers. Perhaps someone you respected once gave you advice that impacted your character, or perhaps someone that you did not respect acted in a certain negative way that you have chosen not to duplicate. Uncover your Being's causes and you uncover You.

Accompanying the Being form of your vessel is a form that acts like a ship travelling toward destinations. This state of "Doing" has also been influenced by many sources, and you may also uncover the influences on your actions using The Wise Questions. Ultimately, you are what you choose to Be and Do…and so is your community. Both forms of you—Being and Doing—exist at the same time, influencing each other as you prioritize each. What fills you? How do you act? What influences do you wish to empty away? What motivations do you wish to keep?

These Being and Doing forms are found throughout our experiences, and even in non-real worlds. Many people enjoy playing video games that allow them to develop the skills and lives of game characters, such as in a game like *The Sims*, or in a movie such as *Avatar*. Even during the control of these imaginary lives, the principle of growth still appears—training develops skill, distractions lengthen the completion of any quest, etc.

These virtual reality experiences suggest our final thought experiment: What you would you do if you could control a life that was real? What if, for 20 years, you could pre-program that life to achieve amazing things because it would stay focused, and not be distracted by short-term "monkey wins?" What would that ultimate "leader," "artist," "analyst," "businessperson," or _____ (fill in the blank)" be like and do? How would they grow physically, emotionally, intellectually, and spiritually?

What if that life was your own?

May you choose to enjoy a real life with lasting happiness and fulfillment, not "monkey wins." When a less successful outcome occurs, may you learn from it and grow. The principle of growth suggests that—

given enough time, training, and effort—all things are possible. Be, Do, and Grow that which you think most worthy of your vessel.

Thank you for your focus. May your ability to accurately predict, decide, and communicate about the future continue to increase in the areas of money, relationships, time, and values.

~ beam, 2012

Additional Principles:

"Big Win," "Not Lose," "Monkey Win"
Effort versus Results
Nice, Provoke-able, & Forgiving

For Further Reflection:

1) If you won a million dollar lottery, what would you Do and Be? Is it really the money that is keeping you from pursuing these "forms?" If so, can you make changes (lesser vehicle, housing, etc.) that will free up the money to allow for this new priority?

2) How might you use your core competencies (areas where you are more cultivated than 80% of the population) to help your community?

3) Growth: Are you performing better than you did two years ago…or have times changed, and those would no longer be good / applicable comparisons (e.g., student income versus post-school income, new knowledge obtained in school versus out of school)? How have you grown since your last birthday…or two birthdays?

4) What part(s) of your parents' marriage would you like to duplicate? Not duplicate?

5) Where do you think you will be in 5 years? Would that change if a romantic partner entered your life, or was no longer a consideration?

6) How would you like to raise children? If boys? If girls? What types of physical, emotional, intellectual, and spiritual upbringing do you think are most important?

7) Are there best times to "surge in a career?" (60-70 hrs/week vs. 40-50 hrs/week) Early, before kids? Always? I have known wives who expect their husbands to work 60+ in order to make CEO, General, etc. Each couple makes their own work priorities…what are yours?

8) What does it mean to "get ahead?" A new car every year? A million dollars saved by age 50? Living on less than you earn? Being able to invest and grow $500 a month? $1000?

9) How would you spend one night per week, or perhaps one afternoon each weekend, doing something that grows you and makes you more interesting?

- Social clubs that build some skill (book club, martial arts, etc.)?
- Charitable work to make a better community (library volunteer, religious youth group coordinator)?
- Other? What do your friends think?

10) What are the truths and limits to a statement such as "If it is good for the individual, it is good for the society"?

11) Are there some issues where you play with a "Big Win" attitude? Harmless board games with friends? Casual flirting where you see who can have the cheesiest pick-up line? What if you have a great business idea? How much risk and uncertainty are you willing to accept? What if this includes failure? Are there some choices where you play "not to lose?" A steady investment plan? A continuous commitment to learning?

12) What do you want to Be and Do? Name 3 steps necessary to arrive there. Compared to how you normally use your money, relationships, time, and values, what changes might you try, and for what intelligent reasons? Can you perform them with a helpful attitude? Do the successful people you know maintain a future focus, or do they get dragged back to the past?

13) What business examples of "enlightened self-interest" and "helping others" have you seen?

14) What are some common "monkey wins" that you have seen? F.L.Y.—A.S.I.A. urges that lead to divorce? Over-eating and under-exercising that leads to obesity? Over-spending that leads to bankruptcy? Valueless people killing others for shoes?

For Further Investigation:

Garrett Hardin *The Tragedy of the Commons*, 1968: http://www.garrethardinsociety.org/articles/art_tragedy_of_the_commons.html

Jared Diamond, *Collapse: How Societies Choose to Fail or Succeed*

Augustine, *The Confessions*

Gary S. Becker, *A Treatise on the Family*

John Gottman, *Why Marriages Succeed or Fail*

Deepak Chopra, *Ageless Body, Timeless Mind*

James Q. Wilson, *The Marriage Problem*

More information on crime, out of wedlock births, and children of single parents can be found at http://www.divorcereform.org/crime.html

Mouse Study: When It Comes To Living Longer, It's Better To Go Hungry Than Go Running, http://www.the-aps.org/press/journal/08/21.htm, Oct '09

Malcolm Ree, James Earles, Mark Teachout, (1994) "Predicting job performance: not much more than g," *Journal of Applied Psychology*

Murray Barrick and Michael Mount, (1991) "The Big Five Personality Dimensions and Job Performance: A Meta-Analysis," *Personnel Psychology*

Thomas Kempis, *The Imitation of Christ*

Robert Axelrod, *The Evolution of Cooperation*

Alexis de Tocqueville, *Democracy in America*

Bennett Galef Jr. (1976). *Social Transmission of Acquired Behavior: A Discussion of Tradition and Social Learning in Vertebrates.*

Will Durant, *The Story of Philosophy*

Father Joseph Koterski, *Natural Law and Human Nature* (www.teach12.com)

Johne E. Finn, *Civil Liberties and the Bill of Rights* (www.teach12.com)

John B Taylor, *Getting Off Track : What Prolonged the Crisis*

William Bennett, *America, The Last Best Hope*

Ayn Rand, *Atlas Shrugged*

The Sims

Avatar

ACKNOWLEDGEMENTS

My initial journeys into the world of free-choice began when I left home for the intellectual treasure of Michigan State University. I thank Andy, Halie, Mark, Heather, Ed, Jennifer, Craig, Sheila, and Tressa for the amazing explorations into how to develop and use one's talents and energies. When I first entered post-school *Life*, I had the good fortune of meeting John, Joe, Dave, Allegra, Joel, and Chris. As budding philosophers and would-be adventurers, we shared and discussed our perspectives on the strengths and weaknesses of our major *Life* decisions. Those insights were priceless.

Long before those worlds of free choice, my Dad adopted me and showed me a powerful approach to achieving contentment, my Mom informed me of the consequences of other journeys, and my Grandma challenged me with many value systems. Both of my brothers considered *Life* choices with me, and my younger brother actually said, "You should write a book first."

More intellectual mentors and colleagues than I could possibly recount further tested and refined my thoughts for this book, including Sifu, Linda, Rita, Kevin, Bill, John, Susan, Chuck, Claudia, Dave, Greeno, Kurt, Toby, T-bone, Big Mike, Owen, Gary, and Rolf. I cannot thank them enough for the insights that each of them has shared with me.

As for the patient and sagacious reviews of my many drafts, I am indebted to the energies of Debbie, Jason, Rachel, Amy, Mike, Carolyn and Nick. Their efforts greatly improved the messages within these pages. Any imperfections are mine alone.

Finally, no testimony of credit and gratitude could ever do justice to the impact of my *Life*-long friend, and world of free choice wife, Karin Anne. With her uplifting warmth and ever adaptive intelligence, she has helped grow my *Life* as well as forge this book. She has been far more than a book editor, partner, or ally. She has been *Life-altering*.

This book is dedicated to my family—blood and chosen…

Made in the USA
San Bernardino, CA
13 February 2014